DAILY READINGS FROM

LIVE
LOVE
LEAD

90 Days of Living Loving Leading

Introduction

If you want to live, love, and lead like Jesus, then I invite you to an adventure of faith over the next 90 days. You can start wherever you are. It's never too late, even if you've taken a few detours and encountered some dead ends along the way. Join me in following the greatest Guide who ever walked the path of life: Jesus.

Living fully, loving completely, leading boldly—these are the hallmarks of Jesus' time on earth. Jesus lived fully present in each moment every day. He gave his attention, his heart, and his energy to those who needed him even as he advanced God's kingdom in the most dramatic way possible. He alone provides us with a model of a big, wide-open life fully lived.

We are all born with God-given potential to change the world around us. But too often we allow our circumstances, disappointments, and doubts to undermine what God wants to do in our lives. Over the next 90 days, if you're willing to spend just a few minutes each day reading, reflecting, and praying through these pages, then you can grow in confidence that despite any setbacks, the path Jesus leads you on is filled with joy, peace, and purpose.

You see, I've learned that it's not always easy to find your way, but Jesus gave us good directions: "Enter by the narrow gate; for wide is the gate and broad is the way that leads to destruction, and there are many who go in by it. Because narrow is the gate and difficult is the way which leads to life, and there are few who find it" (Matt. 7:13–14). This verse has been my road map for most of my life, and I pray that within these pages you will find gathered wisdom and encouragement, often acquired through trial and error, to inspire you along your own path of living, loving, and leading.

We all desire to live a full life, an abundant life, a life over-flowing with purpose and passion. My journey is one of ministry and the Church. Yours may be vastly different. Whether you are in church leadership, business leadership, or—like most of us—involved in family and friendships that require our time and attention, these biblical truths remain consistent across circumstance, challenge, geography, time, or even belief.

Sometimes we have had to make hard decisions and take the road less traveled in order to maintain the purposes to which we felt called. Sometimes our feet may fail as we try to walk through the narrow gate. Especially if we make the passage harder than it needs to be, tighter and more confining. When we allow our fears and insecurities to blind us momentarily, we're often tempted to make the gate narrower than God does. But don't be disheartened. God will always lift us up and sustain us if we're willing. He's promised never to leave us or abandon us on our journey—he's with us for the long haul.

As followers of Christ, we are called to follow in his footsteps, living a big life along a difficult path, journeying through the narrow gate toward a glorious future. God redeems us as his Spirit transforms us, making us more like Jesus each day. While rarely easy or predictable, this process brings more fulfillment to our lives than anything on earth.

Today, I invite you to journey with me and follow in Christ's footsteps. My hope is that your life will be energized and transformed when you encounter his presence and open your heart to all he wants to pour in. My prayer is that you'll find inspiration, hope, and encouragement to break free from all that is holding you back from the exciting, wide-open adventure of faith God has planned for you.

90 Days of Living, Loving, Leading is based on my book, *Live, Love, Lead: Your Best Is Yet to Come!* Each one of these inspirational readings include:

- **Today's Scripture**—A Bible verse or passage that relates to the inspirational reading, giving it a biblical foundation and helping you to understand the truths presented. If you're willing to meditate on these scriptures, you'll be surprised how God will use them to speak to you, direct you, and refresh your spirit.

- **Today's Inspirational Excerpt from *Live, Love, Lead*—** A story, example, or principle that will motivate and inspire you to follow in Jesus' footsteps and grow in your love and dependence on him. These truths are based on my own experience over my years of ministering at Hillsong Church, but more importantly, they're based on God's Word and his promises to us as his children. They will provide fuel for your journey of living, loving, and leading like Jesus.

- **Today's Prayer**—Sometimes it's hard to know what or how to pray on your adventure of faith. So I've provided a basic prayer model to get you started in your conversation with God. Feel free to adapt them to your own life and daily situation, keeping them honest and from your heart. As we're promised in scripture, the effective, fervent prayer of a child of God avails much. There is power in prayer!

- **Today's Reflection on *Living, Loving, Leading*—**As you read each day's inspirational message and prayerfully consider its importance in your own life, take time to journal on what God's Spirit brings to your attention. Meditate on these things, as well as on the way Jesus demonstrates what it means to live fully, love whole-heartedly, and lead boldly.

It is my firm belief that following Jesus is the only journey in life worth taking. After seeing the way God changes hearts, meets impossible needs, heals incurable diseases, and restores people, I am convinced beyond a doubt that God didn't create us to live mediocre, settle-for-less lives. He sent his Son to die on the cross so that we could be forgiven and have eternal life, and not so we could sleepwalk through life as we wait for heaven. The Word of God shows us how to navigate the inevitable twists and turns, and bumps and bruises we may encounter. God has a unique purpose and plan for you—your life, love, and leadership journey was crafted in heaven long before the foundations of the earth.

Your spiritual adventure has already started—and your best is yet to come!

Believing the very best,

Brian Houston

DAY 1
Be Careful What You Dream

Today's Scripture

"For I know the plans I have for you," declares the LORD,
"plans to prosper you and not to harm you,
plans to give you hope and a future."

JEREMIAH 29:11 NIV

When following Jesus, be careful what you dream. Because you can rest assured that God will exceed the limits of your imagination if you're committed to advancing his kingdom. No matter where you are in your life, no matter how many apparent setbacks you face, God's best for you is yet to come. I know firsthand.

If you had met me at age twenty, you would not have nominated me in the "most likely to lead a global ministry" category. Although I was blessed with a loving family—my mum and dad and four siblings—and had grown up active in the church, I felt very awkward as a teenager. I was tall and uncoordinated; I was not a great student and was easily distracted. As I began to follow in my father's footsteps as a pastor and leader, I had to face the fear that so many people have of public speaking. The pressure of being a prominent preacher's son (which no one put on me but myself) caused me to be nervous and insecure, and I blinked incessantly whenever I had to speak in front of people. I didn't stutter, but my eyes did!

But I persevered, learning to relax and to rely on God, because I believed that leading was what God had called me to do. Deep down, I knew I was alive for a purpose bigger than I was, something more important than I could even understand or imagine as a young boy. I was determined that my frequent blinking and self-imposed anxiety would not prevent me from doing what I knew God wanted me to do. At an early age I awakened to the knowledge that God wanted me to serve him in ways that would make a positive difference in people's lives. So gradually, as my faith grew I began to experience his unfolding revelation of what he put me on this earth to do—lead, serve, and equip the local church.

God is working in your life in the same way. He calls each of us to live, love, and lead with whole-hearted abandon to his power and guidance. Your dreams are divine seeds for growing into the person God created you to be.

Today's Thought

Living, loving, and leading like Christ will expand your life, stretch your heart, and deepen your faith.

Today's Prayer

Dear God, I want to follow the example set by your Son, Jesus Christ—to live, love, and lead as he did during his time on earth. Thank you for your many blessings that have brought me to this moment where I am today on my adventure of faith. I know you can do so much more than I can ever do on my own, and I trust that you will use the dreams I have to stretch my faith, open my heart, and deepen my trust in you. Amen.

Today's Reflection on Living, Loving, Leading

_____

_____

_____

_____

_____

_____

_____

_____

_____

_____

_____

_____

_____

_____

_____

_____

_____

_____

_____

_____

_____

_____

_____

_____

_____

_____

_____

_____

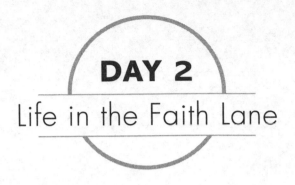

DAY 2
Life in the Faith Lane

Today's Scripture

Now to him who is able to do immeasurably more than all we ask or imagine, according to his power that is at work within us, to him be glory in the church and in Christ Jesus throughout all generations, for ever and ever! Amen.

EPHESIANS 3:20–21 NIV

Living, loving, and leading like Jesus requires us to let go of our own expectations and embrace what God wants to do in our lives today, something I call living in the "faith lane." Too many people try to reduce faith and miracles into quantities, and I don't like trying to evaluate what God is doing by numbers alone. Faith can't be measured in square feet, dollars, and attendance figures. In fact, we remind ourselves regularly that Hillsong Church isn't about the crowd—it's actually all about the *one*. Like the one cabdriver in Guatemala who, with tears in his eyes, told us about the impact of Hillsong music on his broken family. Or the woman in Uganda who discovered we were from Australia and said, "There are only two things I know about Australia: kangaroos and Hillsong!"

Again and again, God has shown me that regardless of the level of success or expansive vision that we have, it all comes back to the lives of individuals. His heart is all about people. So as a result, I honestly see ministry as being about so much more than just numbers. Whether it involves membership, church budgets, weekend attendance, or music sales, I endeavor to look beyond numbers and see transformed lives. The church is not a business or institution; the church is the Body of Christ, alive and attentive to the needs of all people.

It is my belief that most of the evidence of what God is doing goes largely unnoticed and unrecorded. The family reunited after a parent discovers the love of Jesus and completes parole. The divorced person feeling accepted and loved just as she is. The secret addict finding the courage to share his struggle within a community of encouraging believers. The hungry child fed. The lonely widow comforted. The orphan parented. The estranged reconciled. The lost found. Seeing the way God raises the poor from the dust and lifts the needy, seats them on the level of princes, heals the broken, and calls the sinners righteous leaves me with no doubt that following Jesus is the only way to live.

Living in the faith lane isn't a paint-by-numbers picture. It colors outside the lines and sees with different eyes than the world does—eternal eyes with eternal perspective. It requires living by faith, day by day and step by step.

Today's Thought

Your Heavenly Father didn't create you to live a life of mediocrity.
He created you to live life in the faith lane.

Today's Prayer

Dear Heavenly Father, continue to show me the needs of the people around me, reminding me of your love for them. I never want to lose my focus on what you're doing in the lives of individuals or become distracted by quantity over quality in my ministry. Thank you for calling me to live in the faith lane, following in the footsteps of Jesus rather than settling for a safe path of mediocrity. Amen.

Today's Reflection on Living, Loving, Leading

_____

_____

_____

DAY 3
Walking on Water

Today's Scripture

Then Peter got down out of the boat,
walked on the water, and came toward Jesus.
But when he saw the wind, he was afraid and,
beginning to sink, cried out, "Lord, save me!"

MATTHEW 14:29–30 NIV

Living in the faith lane is not necessarily life in the fast lane. Instead of driving, maybe living in the faith lane is more like swimming. I've spent a great deal of my life near the water on the great beaches of Australia, swimming or simply enjoying a coffee at a beachside café. This sunburned country is the biggest island in the world, which means we have more coastline than anywhere else. My native New Zealand is composed of islands as well, and as a boy, there was nothing I loved more than being at the beach, floating in the cool water, finding relief from the summer heat.

But living in the faith lane is much more than just floating along, letting life's current carry you wherever it wants. Living in the faith lane is about taking control of your future while still depending on Jesus for every step you take—even when that means walking on water. Too often, we tend to respond like Peter when we find ourselves in the midst of a storm.

A scrappy fisherman by trade, Peter can't believe his eyes when he and his fellow disciples look up and see someone treading the choppy waters toward them. Is it a ghost? Or could it really be their Master?

Peter wants proof. "If it's really you, Lord," he shouts into the howling wind, "then tell me to come to you on the water!"

"Come!" Christ yells back.

And then it happens. Peter gets out of the boat and takes a step.

He's walking on water.

But then Peter notices the wind picking up again and he panics. Maybe he starts thinking, "I'm walking on water! Wait a minute—that's impossible! Can't be done!"

Yes, walking on water is impossible—unless you have faith. The kind that Peter had for those moments as he simply obeyed the Lord's command. The kind that he had before he started thinking about why he could not do what he was doing. The kind you have when you're living in the faith lane.

What is it that's ahead of you right now that feels impossible? What is the "middle of the storm, walk on water" task in front of you that feels immediately daunting and impossibly fearful?

Today's Thought

At some point, we all need faith to step out of the boat
and take that first step.

Today's Prayer

Dear Jesus, I'm often frightened by the storms of life and don't know where to turn. Remind me of your presence during those times and your ability to calm the tides churning around me. Help me to remember that you not only walked on water, but you also call me to follow you and do the same. What seems impossible to me is more than possible with you. Amen.

Today's Reflection on Living, Loving, Leading

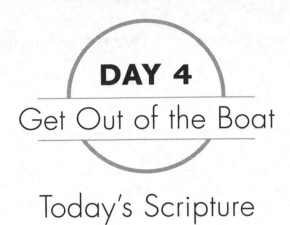

DAY 4

Get Out of the Boat

Today's Scripture

Jesus replied, "What is impossible with man is possible with God."

LUKE 18:27 NIV

So often we fail because we get stuck in our heads, tangled in our thoughts, mired in speculation and probability, grasping to make life work any way we can. We want to walk on water. But we insist on trying to do it under our own power. If we put our trust in something else—technology to control the weather, money for a bigger boat, or a life vest "just in case"—then maybe we can figure it out. But we can't! The moment we think we can is when we take our eyes off Jesus—and that's when we begin to sink!

If you want to live, love, and lead like Jesus, then there's no other place to live but in the faith lane. To discover his plan for your life, you will need to step into the great unknown, risking everything you have. If you get out of the boat and follow the sound of his voice, you will take steps you never thought possible.

I've experienced this process of getting out of the boat time and time again as my wife, Bobbie, and I have pastored Hillsong Church. If you could see the little school hall where we first held church services before we moved to a vacant warehouse surrounded by fields on the northwest outskirts of Sydney, then you would marvel just as we do. If you could see me washing shopwindows to make ends meet or see Bobbie getting up early to help set up chairs for our service, then you would begin to grasp what God has done.

All we had to do was continue to get out of the boat. If you want to live, love, and lead like Jesus, then there's no other place to live but in the faith lane. To discover his plan for your life, you will need to step into the great unknown, risking everything you have. If you get out of the boat and follow the sound of his voice, you will take steps you never thought possible.

You will begin a mystery tour, an excursion to his unspecified destinations. You will come alive with the possibility of relying on God to do what seems impossible. You will find yourself challenged, stretched, and tried and tested. You may even walk on water.

Today's Thought

Life is a journey, a winding path filled with many unknowns.
It's only possible to navigate because of God's power and grace.

Today's Prayer

*Dear Lord, I often try to make life work on my own efforts,
attempting to control areas that frighten me and seem unmanageable.
Thank you that you have already gone before me and blazed a trail,
guiding me out of my comfort zone and into the abundant,
wide-open, spacious life you came to bring. May I always
remember that you have everything under control,
even when it doesn't feel that way. Amen.*

Today's Reflection on Living, Loving, Leading

_____

_____

_____

_____

_____

DAY 5
Effortless Grace

Today's Scripture

For by grace you have been saved through faith.
And this is not your own doing; it is the gift of God,
not a result of works, so that no one may boast.

EPHESIANS 2:8–9 ESV

I love mornings at home in Sydney when I have ample time to get up and about. When I wake up on those days, it's usually quite early, so I rummage around in the dark in a vain attempt not to wake Bobbie. I'm bleary-eyed and still half-asleep, but my routine is so familiar I don't have to think about it. I find my Nike T-shirt, some basketball shorts, my running shoes, and my favorite old cap. While the other items might get commandeered by my wife for the laundry bin, it's the same cap every day.

I go for a walk, maybe a slow jog, and end up reading the paper over coffee at my favorite beachside café. Then I think, plan, daydream, and pray about what's ahead in my schedule. These slow, stay-at-home preparation mornings are my favorite, because I can stay in my favorite, most comfortable clothes.

You probably have your own special items that have become your favorites over the years: a pair of old jeans, a leather jacket, a concert T-shirt, or a first-date dress. Such pieces not only fit like a glove but they're also very comfortable. You feel good wearing them.

Don't you wish your life felt as comfortable as your favorite clothes? That you felt just as comfortable in your own skin as you do in your favorite pair

23

of jeans? That your life expressed the alignment of who you are with who God made you to be?

I'm convinced that we all long for this kind of life. We see it displayed sometimes by individuals who discover their calling, embrace it fully, and then excel at levels off the chart. People living in this gracious rhythm that combines their passion, talents, abilities, and opportunities seem to stand out. We admire their achievements and are inspired by their contributions to others around them, the way they love living life and do it with seemingly effortless grace.

But you don't have to sit on the sidelines and envy the lives of others. God created you for a specific purpose and calls you to discover the deeper satisfaction that comes from living, loving, and leading like Jesus. This is the joy of a wide-open, abundant life lived in the faith lane, stepping out and following our Savior.

Today's Thought

When we're aligned with our God-given abilities and
purpose, we experience the same kind of effortless grace
we see in those who excel around us—the kind of life
that's as comfortable as our favorite clothes.

Today's Prayer

*Dear God, I often make the life of faith harder than it has to
be, trying to live up to the expectations of others or attempting to
earn your favor. Thank you for your unconditional love, limitless
grace, and infinite mercy. Allow me to experience the comfort
of your presence throughout my day today, that relaxed,
effortless feeling of trusting you. Amen.*

Today's Reflection on Living, Loving, Leading

_____

_____

_____

_____

_____

_____

_____

_____

_____

_____

_____

_____

_____

_____

_____

_____

_____

_____

DAY 6
Overwhelmed

Today's Scripture

"My grace is sufficient for you, for my power is made perfect in weakness." Therefore I will boast all the more gladly of my weaknesses, so that the power of Christ may rest upon me.

2 CORINTHIANS 12:9 ESV

Recently, my wife Bobbie and I were driving along in the car, chatting about various matters, before lapsing into that comfortable silence you enjoy with someone you love. Then Bobbie turned to me suddenly and said, "Do you ever feel overwhelmed?"

Knowing our big women's conference was quickly approaching, along with the many other people and concerns she was juggling in her heart, I knew exactly where her question was coming from. As soon as she asked the question, without hesitating I answered, "All the time."

To be honest, we've never known a time when we haven't felt out of our depth. When we were young, we didn't have the resources or the experience to feel confident in what we were doing, so we had to rely on God each and every day. Then when we got a few years under our belt, both our family and our church family began growing and developing, and this always kept us on our toes, improvising under God's grace, looking to him for guidance, provision, and protection.

Then, as he has entrusted more responsibilities and resources to us, we feel even more overwhelmed. But God has been more than faithful in providing all we've needed and more. But it's never been through our own power, talents, abilities, or influence. It's only through his grace.

Perhaps you, too, can feel overwhelmed. Maybe you feel trapped, caught in a cycle of tasks and bills and deadlines and not enough hours in the day. Life is certainly full of overwhelming moments, especially for those of us who want to do something worthwhile with our lives, to live with a sense of purpose. Yet we don't have to rely on our power.

The Bible has so much to say about living in grace—knowing, walking, and living in the undeserved favor of a kind and merciful God. The Bible is full of characters who felt out of their depth at times, inadequate for the task placed in front of them. People like Mephibosheth, who was a foreigner in a king's house. Moses, who was slow in speech. David, who was just a mere shepherd boy. Even a prostitute named Rahab, who was asked to betray her own people in order to save her family and trust a God she barely knew.

Time and time again, no matter who it is, they were all overwhelmed. And yet God gave them sufficient grace to fulfill their unique purpose and calling. I have to trust he does the same for you and me today.

Today's Thought

The demands of life are overwhelming unless you rely on the sufficiency of God's daily grace. When you're following in his footsteps, he always provides what you need right when you need it.

Today's Prayer

Dear Lord Jesus, I often feel overwhelmed by all the responsibilities, duties, and obligations in my life. I know that living, loving, and leading like you may not be easy, but it will never require more than you provide—your power, your resources, your support. Your sense of timing is better than mine, and I can relax by trusting you when I feel pulled in every direction. In you, I have all I need. Amen.

Today's Reflection on Living, Loving, Leading

_____

_____

_____

_____

_____

_____

_____

_____

_____

_____

_____

_____

_____

_____

_____

_____

_____

_____

_____

_____

_____

_____

DAY 7
Your Own Sphere of Grace

Today's Scripture

I praise you because I am fearfully and wonderfully made;
your works are wonderful, I know that full well.

PSALM 139:14 NIV

I remember clearly the first ever ministry trip that Bobbie and I took together to America. We were invited to speak at a conference on the West Coast, and Bobbie and I were feeling a bit unsure, because it was our first time ministering in the United States. We had heard some things about ministry in the United States, like "pastors' wives only wear skirts" and none of the other speakers there had a ponytail like I did. We arrived feeling a bit sensitive about our "Australian-isms," and I remember sitting and listening to the other conference speakers so eloquently teaching in their polished American accents and thinking to myself, "What am *I* doing here?!" Yet it was the words of one of our good friends in ministry that brought me back to reality. As I was getting up to speak, he patted me on the back and said, "Brian, just be yourself. Be Australian—that's why we love you!"

To this day, while I am entirely comfortable and confident in who I am, there are still times when I can momentarily feel out of my depth. During these moments, I remember the example set by the apostle Paul. While each person's story in the Bible gives us clues about how to live in the comfort of our own grace, Paul speaks of it directly.

In almost every letter he wrote, whether to the Romans, the Ephesians, the Colossians, or whoever, he begins by introducing himself within the context of grace. In each case he exudes a clear confidence and natural strength,

DAILY READINGS FROM LIVE LOVE LEAD

a real ease with himself. He has lost his limitations and instead focuses on what he's been called to do, trusting in God's power to accomplish it.

Notice how he begins his letter to the Ephesians: "Paul, an apostle of Jesus Christ by the will of God, to the saints who are in Ephesus" (Eph. 1:1). It seems a natural way to begin a letter, I suppose, but if you stop and consider it, his confidence shines through. Paul basically says, "Paul—*this is who I am. An apostle—this is what I do. Of Jesus Christ—this is who I do it for. By the will of God—this is my authority. To the saints who are in Ephesus—this* is my audience." In one brief sentence, Paul has revealed his entire sphere of grace!

Today's Thought

We can be so distracted by our own insecurities, trying to fit
into the boxes of other people's expectations and putting pressure
on ourselves to be someone different, that we forget who we are.
We must remember: God created us to be authentic and unique,
not a copy of anyone else but our Master's original.
He gives each of us our own sphere of grace.

Today's Prayer

*Dear God, I give you praise and glory for making me so unique
and special. Today I ask that you would remind me that I don't need
to compare myself to anyone else and that I don't have to strive to be
something or someone I'm not. Your Word tells me I am fearfully
and wonderfully made. I have my own sphere of grace
in which to live, love, and lead. Amen.*

Today's Reflection on Living, Loving, Leading

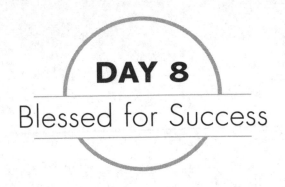

DAY 8

Blessed for Success

Today's Scripture

*But to each one of us grace has been given
as Christ apportioned it.*

EPHESIANS 4:7 NIV

By living out his own special measure of grace, Paul accomplished amazing things for the kingdom of God. He reached across most of the world known to exist in his time with the good news of the gospel. He wrote letters of truth given by God's Spirit to inform, to instruct, and to inspire generations of readers and believers. He faced danger and stared down death on many occasions, and he was calm and centered in the midst of storms, shipwrecks, hostile crowds, and prison riots.

Just as Paul personalized the grace he had been given, you must embrace the grace God has given you. When you live inside your own sphere of grace, when you lose the limitations of living up to anyone else's expectations, then you become comfortable with yourself and your life in a way that feels like putting on your favorite clothes.

When you live within the parameters of your own special grace, then life feels open and expansive. You stop comparing and start appreciating. The abundant life Jesus came to bring us frees us from the confines of culture, competition, and comparison. We can be generous, inclusive, and grace filled, enjoying the fulfillment of our purpose as we love others just as we are loved.

When you're living the full, abundant, wide-open life for which you were designed, everything you do will be characterized by passion, purpose, perspective, and peace. You'll be excited to wake up each morning, eager to get out of bed and get on with the day that the Lord has made and set before you. Hard work and unexpected obstacles won't deter you or frustrate you for long, because you know you're doing what you were made to do, being your most authentic self, liberated by the grace of God.

God has dealt each one of us a measure of grace. That measure is *all* you need to fulfill the purpose of God in your life. It may sound a bit farfetched or oversimplified, but each one of us is born with uniquely tailored gifts and latent abilities, individually matched to our own unique purpose in life. Discovering this fact and living in the power of it is what will release you into a large and expansive life—a life you perhaps could only ever dream of, that you thought was just for the lucky ones. The key to the future you hope for is found in being faithful with the measure God has given *you*.

Today's Thought

When we live out of the free, unmerited favor of God,
we discover his grace is all-encompassing and all-sufficient.
His grace provides an answer to every problem, a way
through any obstacle, an enabling power to do
what we cannot do in our own power.

Today's Prayer

*Dear God, today I ask that you would grant me a new
and clearer understanding of grace, especially the unique
measure of grace I've been given. I pray I would never take
advantage of your grace and continue knowingly to sin.
But I also pray I would not linger on my sins when you have
forgiven me and blessed me with this special portion
of your life-giving grace. Amen.*

Today's Reflection on Living, Loving, Leading

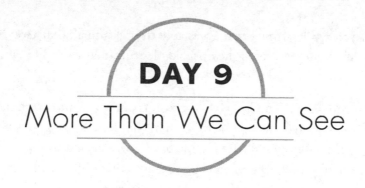

DAY 9
More Than We Can See

Today's Scripture

*I am confident of this, that the one who began
a good work among you will bring it to
completion by the day of Jesus Christ.*

PHILIPPIANS 1:6 NRSV

I was five years old when I made the decision to accept Jesus as my Lord and Savior. As long as I can remember, all I wanted to do was pastor a church and be a part of building God's kingdom. After I finished school, I went to Bible college and then began to serve in the local church wherever I could. Today, with more than forty years in ministry behind me, I am living my dream, and the passion to serve God burns stronger than ever. Yet I didn't always live in the knowledge or the understanding of my appointed sphere, understanding my strengths, embracing my weaknesses, and discovering my grace zone. There were many times when I seriously questioned myself and doubted whether in fact I could really do the things I longed to.

I can still remember being in Bible college at eighteen years old. There was a time when each student had to give a short devotional talk to the other students, maybe sixty or seventy people. The moment came for me to speak, and to this day I remember deliberately walking out the door, getting in my car, and driving in the opposite direction just so I wouldn't have to speak in front of them!

Today, I regularly stand before great crowds of people in large arenas, comfortably delivering a forty-minute message—but that was not always the case! It was when I became comfortable in myself, when I listened to what

35

God had to say about me, that I was able to step into all that God had for me. It was then I discovered the unshakable truth that you will never come second by putting God first.

I remain convinced that God gives each of us our own grace, a special measure of blessings that line up exactly with his purposes for our lives. Sadly, it took longer than it should have for me to discover my grace zone—and yet I have realized that it is never too late to start living in that realm of reality. God always sees more in us than we can see in ourselves.

God's plans for you are *always* bigger than you are, and they are never going to be something you can pull off easily and in your own strength. But when you live in your grace zone, you will be amazed at what he will do through you.

Today's Thought

God's plans for you are *always* bigger than you are, and they are never going to be something you can pull off easily and in your own strength. But when you live in your grace zone, you will be amazed at what he will do through you.

Today's Prayer

Dear Lord, sometimes I struggle with my self-confidence, either feeling insecure and unsure of myself and my abilities or else being proud and even boastful. Please remind me that my confidence comes from you so that I might remain both humble and strong as I follow you today. Thank you that I don't need to worry or rely on my own abilities because you are so much bigger than my own efforts. Amen.

Today's Reflection on Living, Loving, Leading

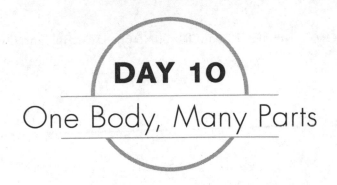

DAY 10
One Body, Many Parts

Today's Scripture

For as we have many members in one body, but all the members do not have the same function, so we, being many, are one body in Christ, and individually members of one another. Having then gifts differing according to the grace that is given to us, let us use them.

ROMANS 12:4–6 NKJV

God isn't schizophrenic. He didn't create you one way, in order to use you another way. He knew exactly what he had in mind for your future when he formed you. The verses above give us a glimpse into the way God has designed each of us individually, to function in the measure or sphere with which he has uniquely appointed us.

What are your strengths? Can you identify the unique giftings that are on your life? Because they are there, whether you recognize them or not. It is easy to fill your mind with what you do not have and lose sight of what God can do with what you *do* have. Some people are uniquely graced for business, others for ministry or for motherhood, and the list goes on! Perhaps you are graced with the gift of generosity or the gift of compassion—a heart that breaks for the hurting and the needy. What a beautiful gift to have!

We're told, "As each one has received a gift, minister it to one another, as good stewards of the manifold grace of God" (1 Pet. 4:10). Here *manifold* literally means the "many-fold" or "many-layered," the "multidimensional" grace of God. Whether you are graced with the gift of leadership, the gift of athletics, or the gift of creativity, we are called to be good stewards and faithful servants of what is in our hand. No one is exempt, and if you didn't play your part we would be missing out on the unique grace and the individual strengths that you bring to the here and now.

Knowing the measure of grace God has given you means you don't have to be somebody else. It's so liberating! You don't have to try to achieve any milestone or award to feel self-confident. You just have to be faithful with the measure of grace God has given you.

There is a beautiful satisfaction that comes from knowing that we are doing exactly what God made us to do and are being obedient to his calling on our lives. It is as we discover our strengths, and grow comfortable in the grace we have been given, that we will begin to see the promises of God for our wide-open, spacious future begin to take shape.

Today's Thought

Faithfulness means holding on to your purpose and trusting in God's goodness in the midst of all the peaks, celebrations, and mountaintops, as well as the trials, temptations, and tragedies that life throws at you. This is how you grow, grounded in grace.

Today's Prayer

Dear Heavenly Father, I praise you for your goodness and mercy today, for the unique gifts with which you've blessed me. Today please open my eyes so that I may see the needs of others that you want to meet through my abilities. Use my strengths to bless others, God, so they may see your love and grace through all I do. Amen.

Today's Reflection on Living, Loving, Leading

DAY 11

Agree to Disagree

Today's Scripture

"Again I say to you that if two of you agree on earth
concerning anything that they ask, it will be done
for them by My Father in heaven. For where two
or three are gathered together in My name,
I am there in the midst of them."

MATTHEW 18:19–20 NKJV

I've got four granddaughters, two grandsons, six in all. I'm "that guy" when it comes to my grandkids—you don't dare ask me a question about them without being bombarded by photos and forced to listen to stories of their latest achievements and daily adventures. Being their "Pops" is one of my greatest joys. I used to tease my kids that I wanted them to have enough grandchildren to form my own rugby team, but these days it's looking more likely that I might end up with a ballet troupe.

I enjoy watching how they relate to one another. Three of them are old enough to be approaching school age and play together frequently, two sisters and one cousin. Any two of them seem to get along quite well, sharing silly stories and giggling, but when a third joins in, then things become a bit chaotic. The old adage "Two's company and three's a crowd" is actually quite true in my experience.

Two of them can usually play together contentedly enough. However, when a third joins in, there's often a shift in the balance of power. Someone is bound to be left out. One wants something another one has, who in turn wants something the third one holds.

41

Such is the way of the world. We can get a small group of like-minded people to agree with us, but bring in someone who's significantly different than we are and the dynamic changes. Scripture directly addresses this relational dynamic in the verses above. And it's interesting to me that this passage speaks of two agreeing, but three *gathering*.

Obviously, the more people that gather, the more difficult agreement becomes. When there is a crowd, we may agree on some things but we are not going to agree on everything. When you begin factoring in each of our individual backgrounds, special interests, and personal agendas, it's amazing how much we can disagree on—or that we can agree together on anything!

I'm convinced our fellowship with one another cannot be based merely on agreement. It must be based on Jesus, and on the love that he so readily gives to each and every person who calls on his name. This is the only way we can love one another as he has loved us.

Today's Thought

In order to love the people around us—especially those who
may be radically different than we are—we often have to agree
to disagree. Only the love of Christ has the power
to unite people in the midst of conflict.

Today's Prayer

*Dear Jesus, I confess that relationships can be a struggle for me
at times. I want to love those around me with your kind of
unconditional love, but so often I fail and get caught up in petty
disagreements. I pray today your Spirit would guide me and keep me
sensitive to the people in my life. Help me remember it's okay to agree
to disagree about the small stuff in order that we can focus
on your truth and the big life we've been given. Amen.*

Today's Reflection on Living, Loving, Leading

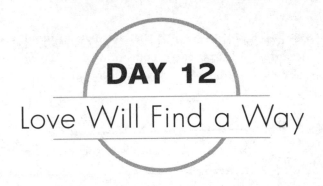

DAY 12

Love Will Find a Way

Today's Scripture

*For the kingdom of God is not a matter of
eating and drinking, but of righteousness,
peace and joy in the Holy Spirit.*

ROMANS 14:17 NIV

A few years ago I was approached by a major news outlet in Australia with an opportunity to support our state rugby league team before the biggest match of the year, one they had lost many years in a row. So as requested, I did a photo shoot in our team's jersey alongside other religious leaders, next to a headline that urged sports fans to "Keep the Faith."

It was a fun article and one I happily and playfully went along with, tossing a footie around with my new acquaintance, a local Muslim imam. Did he and I agree on the fundamentals of faith and religion? Of course not—we are poles apart! But do we both support the same football team and light-heartedly pray for a miracle victory? *Yes!*

Sadly, as Christians, we can be so much quicker to build walls than we are to build bridges. This is not about compromising your beliefs; it is simply about loving the very people whom Jesus gave his life for. Jesus was the master of crossing divides. He crossed gender divides, cultural divides, moral divides, and doctrinal and political divides.

There's a world full of people out there with whom I don't agree and many of them don't agree with what I'm all about. When it comes to ethics and morality, many unchurched people might disagree with where I stand. Often people who have points of disagreement can be very passionate about their views. It seems these days that any person in authority who is building something significant has a collection of naysayers and bloggers ready to cut down and criticize anything and everything that they disagree with. Yet I believe we have to find a way to love other people beyond our disagreements.

I have always been firm in the belief that Hillsong Church and our ministry was going to be built on the things that we are for, and not on what we are against. We are for Jesus. We are for love. We are for his grace and forgiveness, for the healing and wholeness and transformed lives that come with saying yes to a relationship with Christ. We are for seeing you rise up, loosen shackles and shame built up by condemnation, and enter into a life of fulfillment and purpose—the life you were created to live.

—————————————— O ——————————————

Today's Thought

Even when we don't know how we can love someone so different from us, if we rely on the love of God, then we will find a way.

Today's Prayer

Dear God, today I pray you would allow me to build bridges and not walls with people who are different from me. Whether they have different beliefs, a different culture, or a different lifestyle than my own, I thank you that I can still show them the love of Jesus without compromising your truth. We are all your children on this earth, and we all need a Savior. Thank you that your love always finds a way. Amen.

Today's Reflection on Living, Loving, Leading

_____

_____

_____

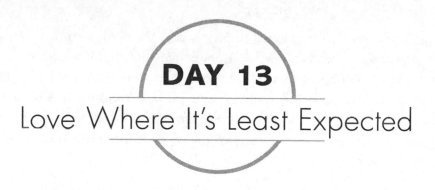

DAY 13

Love Where It's Least Expected

Today's Scripture

Walk in love, just as Christ loved us and gave himself up for us as a fragrant offering and sacrifice to God.

EPHESIANS 5:2 NIV

If you want to love the way Jesus loved, if you want your life to be characterized by love in a way that reflects the heart of God to everyone you meet, then I recommend paying attention to how you respond to people who make you uncomfortable. You know, the ones who are different from you in significant ways, the ones you don't like, don't understand, and don't enjoy. The people who hold different beliefs, practice different lifestyles, and hold distinctly different priorities from your own.

While there are many different dimensions to Christian love, I believe the ability to love unconditionally is the one that most characterizes the spacious, abundant life we have in Christ. And I suspect this willingness to love others unconditionally and its regular practice are what's significantly missing from many believers' lives. We say we want to love others just as God loves us, but too often we end up choosing comfort and convenience over compassion. This is not the example set by Christ and not the way we are called to love.

As painful as relationships can sometimes be, we are made in God's image as relational beings, created to belong, to serve, to worship, and to live in community. God often provides for us and loves us through the people in our lives even as we're called to be his hands and feet to those around us. Relationships are the lifeblood of the Church, the Body of Christ.

Yet, we're continually tempted to play it safe. We don't mean to become insular and self-righteous, exclusive and judgmental, but if we don't focus on our relationship with God foremost, then we're prone to becoming proud. We want to love all people, but unless we're consistently experiencing the love of Christ in our lives every day, then we end up trying to do it on our own. And the love required to love people different from us will always be supernatural.

As a result of his unconditional love for all people, we often find God in the midst of places and situations where we least expect him. On the street corners and in alleyways. In the hospitals and prisons, orphanages and courtrooms. Everywhere you find people, there you will also find God. His love is often most powerful in places where it's least expected.

Today's Thought

Jesus calls us to love others wherever we find them, especially in unpleasant and unfamiliar places, to stretch ourselves beyond what's convenient and comfortable.

Today's Prayer

Dear Lord Jesus, I pray you would give me the courage, strength, and compassion to love those people who may criticize, condemn, or challenge me today. Give me your patience and peace, your sense of seeing their unique worth as another son or daughter of your Heavenly Father. Thank you for providing an example of what it means to love people who are not easy to love. Amen.

Today's Reflection on Living, Loving, Leading

_____

_____

_____

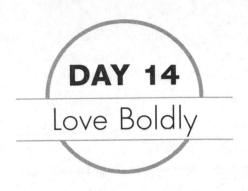

DAY 14
Love Boldly

Today's Scripture

"For God did not send His Son into the world to condemn the world, but that the world through Him might be saved."

JOHN 3:17 NKJV

Paul the apostle began his career as an angry Jewish legalist devoted to persecuting these upstart radicals who followed Jesus. It was only after Paul encountered Christ so directly and dramatically on his journey to Damascus that he discovered the fullness of living in God's grace, free to be himself as his Father created him and free to love others. As Saul, he was controlling, closed-minded, and driven by his own ego, but as God's beloved apostle, Paul became accepting, openhearted, and driven by his love for this God who had first loved him.

Paul discovered the message of grace that sets us all free: Jesus didn't come to condemn the world but to save it. If God wanted to condemn the world, he would have sent a condemner. But he wanted to save the world, so he sent us a Savior as we see in the verse above (John 3:17).

In fact, if you notice how Jesus treated the various people he encountered during his time on earth, the contrast is quite striking. Jesus kept his harshest words for the religious bullies he encountered—and reached out to sinners and publicans, all with a measure of love and grace, in order that they might be saved. An adulterous woman, a serial divorcee (now living with another man), a Samaritan woman, a small-time con man, and a tax collector that he called down from a tree were among those he loved and treated with grace.

What frames the tone of your life? How often do you stretch beyond your comfort zone to reach out to people whom you are in disagreement with? The ability to enjoy a big, spacious, openhearted life is directly proportional to your ability to love everyone, especially those who are different from you.

What are your expectations of God regarding how you are to love others? What would you do if God called you into a place you didn't like or a situation that you disregarded? Would you struggle and suffer with your own prejudices and biases in order to share God's abundant love and merciful grace to people whom you dislike? God loves us without conditions, though too often we place conditions on our love before extending it to others.

We cannot reduce people's whole lives into one sweeping, judgmental statement filled with condemnation. Jesus never did that, and we must look at their issues through gracious eyes—through Jesus' eyes.

Today's Thought

It's easy to judge others and condemn them for their
sinful behavior. However, in order to love others with the bold
love of Jesus, you must confront your biases, prejudices,
and fears about other people.

Today's Prayer

*Dear God, search me and show me the biases and prejudices I
have in my heart, the attitudes about others that prevent me from
loving them with the fullness of your love. Forgive me for the
ways I have been unkind or indifferent to those who are different
from me. Today help me face my fears and uncertainties about
those differences and trust that all people have more in
common than what keeps us apart. Amen.*

Today's Reflection on Living, Loving, Leading

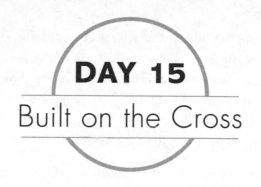

DAY 15
Built on the Cross

Today's Scripture

May I never boast except in the cross of our Lord Jesus Christ, through which the world has been crucified to me, and I to the world.

GALATIANS 6:14 NIV

As we seek to love others with the love of Christ, I believe we are bound by the Word we live by, the world we live in, and the weight we live with. Let me explain. The Word we live by is obviously the Word of God. I cannot and would not want to unwrite the Bible. Yet the world we live in is continuously changing. I don't believe it is our job as Christians to squeeze the Word of God into the mold of the world, but it is our job to love the world that Jesus died for and it is our commission to reach all people. And the weight we live with is a heavy one.

Many churches, whether you choose to acknowledge it or not, have young people who are growing up in good Christian families and yet are struggling with confusing issues of identity. Tragically, when they have tried to bring their struggles to trusted confidences, like youth pastors and friends, they have instead been alienated and ostracized. Perhaps well-meaning parents, who simply haven't known what to do, have sown words of rejection into their children's most vulnerable moments. The consequences of this are that time and time again we have seen these young people—who were once grounded and planted in church—end up hating God and despising every form of organized religion.

I care about young lives. I care about their futures, and the answer isn't

53

compromising the Scriptures, but it is also not about reducing people's lives into unloving statements. It's about seeing what God sees—and loving others with the same unconditional love we have been shown by our Savior, Jesus Christ. People from all walks of life are welcome at our church, and I pray that when people walk through the doors they all feel a sense of welcome home. For "whosoever will to the Lord may come."

That doesn't mean that people don't need to change. The Christian message is a message of transformation, and we are all sinners saved by grace. Yes—God wants us to change, and God helps us to change, but like Billy Graham said, "It is the Holy Spirit's job to convict, God's job to judge, and my job to love."

Today's Thought

Our world is full of disagreement. But thank God that our loving acceptance of people doesn't have to be built on agreeing with them. Our loving acceptance of them is built on the cross.

Today's Prayer

Dear Father God, you lovingly accept all people where they are. None of us is perfect and will ever be completely free of sin in this life. Thank you that you accept me just as I am today— struggles, weaknesses, and all. May I show this same attitude of loving acceptance to people with whom I may disagree or find uncomfortable. Give me courage to love them boldly, to surprise them with your grace. Amen.

Today's Reflection on Living, Loving, Leading

_____

_____

_____

Today's Scripture

"All authority in heaven and on earth has been given to me.
Therefore go and make disciples of all nations."

MATTHEW 28:18–19 NIV

Not long ago we gave our entire church wristbands with the words "Missio Dei" on them. The back of the bracelet was meant to have the translation on it—"Mission of God"—but when we received well over forty thousand bracelets from our manufacturer in China, the engraving said, "Missio Dei, Mission of COD"! You have to laugh at it now, but at the time it caused a bit of anxiety for our communications and events teams!

The bracelets were to serve as a daily reminder for our church that each day we wake up we are "on mission," co-heirs with Christ and missionaries to the world around us. And to complete our mission it is important that we deal with the very things that may be holding us back or standing in the way of our connection with others.

You and I are certainly not the only ones who struggle with loving people who are different than we are. Jesus' disciples faced this challenge as well, as did most people in the early Church. So much of Jewish religious law and cultural customs were based on rigid boundaries between what was holy and what was impure, what was sacred and what was common, what was pure and what was unclean. Elaborate rituals were carried out in order for a person to cleanse himself, and make himself worthy to enter the temple and present an offering to the Lord before the priests.

The Israelites knew they were God's chosen people. They had seen God lead them, protect them, and set them apart from other tribes and other nations. They were used to thinking of themselves as the only people God loved and favored. Such was the world of Palestine during Christ's lifetime.

However, Jesus came for all people, not just the nation of Israel. This was one of the most radical aspects of his message, the good news that anyone could be forgiven of their sins and have a relationship with their Heavenly Father. And Christ made it clear how important it was to take this message beyond the city limits of Jerusalem and the borders of Israel.

We call this message the Great Commission, the co-mission we have to tell others about the love of God and how he manifested it by sending his Son to die on a cross for our sins. This message is the heart of God for all of his people. It always has been and always will be. When we encounter the Lord's mercy, grace, and forgiveness, his love for us becomes abundantly clear. Consequently, we can't wait to share it with others.

Today's Thought

Align yourself with God's mission of grace, the Great Commission. Step up and recognize the opportunity among your everyday encounters to love people with an extraordinary, unconditional love.

Today's Prayer

Dear Jesus, today I ask that you would impress on my heart the urgency of taking the good news of the gospel to all people, not just the ones I like or find easy to be with. Show me the opportunities you're opening for me so that I may step out in faith and let others know who you are and all you've done for me and people everywhere. Remind me what it means to love the way you love. Amen.

Today's Reflection on Living, Loving, Leading

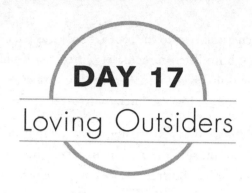

DAY 17
Loving Outsiders

Today's Scripture

Then Peter opened his mouth and said: "In truth I perceive that God shows no partiality. But in every nation whoever fears Him and works righteousness is accepted by Him. The word which God sent to the children of Israel, preaching peace through Jesus Christ—He is Lord of all—that word you know."

ACTS 10:34–37 NKJV

One of the greatest examples of unconditional love that crossed every kind of cultural and social divide is found in Acts 10. It's the story of two men whose worlds were far apart. One is Cornelius, a young centurion in the Roman army. As a Roman gentile, and in terms of the Jewish religious law, he was an outsider. He was considered unclean and common, a soldier required to kill, and yet the Bible tells us that Cornelius loved God. And then there's Peter, a young Jewish man, bound by Jewish law, who also defied the expectations of others. An untrained, uneducated fisherman, Peter was known to be a disciple of Jesus Christ.

Although these two are polar opposites, God gives them both separate dreams, preparing them for a meeting that changed history. Staying at the house of Simon the Tanner, in itself an impure place a Jew should never have entered, Peter receives an invitation from Cornelius' servants.

Knowing he was outside conventional boundaries, Peter might have been uncomfortable; he might even have been a little afraid. But Peter went where God directed him and acknowledged the all-inclusive, unconditional love shown by Christ on the cross: we are all sinners saved by grace.

59

And as soon as Peter walked into the room, Cornelius fell to the ground and started to worship him. Peter immediately lifted the Roman soldier to his feet and said something like "Get up, man! I'm no better than you. Stand up and look me in the eye because I'm a man just like you" (see Acts 10:26).

Peter went on to explain that yes, usually Jewish people did not mingle with foreigners and those outside the nation of Israel; however, God showed Peter that he was to accept outsiders and share the gospel with them. Since Cornelius had gathered many relatives, friends, and servants at his home in order to meet Peter, he was overjoyed at such acceptance.

You and I are called to treat people perceived to be outsiders with the same respect Peter showed Cornelius. We may disagree with their lifestyles, their morals, their principles, their religious beliefs, but the love required to fuel the big, spacious life modeled by Jesus always invites others to the party. If we're honest, none of us are going to agree on everything all the time. We can only agree on the one name with the power to save our souls: Jesus Christ.

Today's Thought

Don't live in a world full of disagreement, trying to prove
yourself right all the time. Don't exclude others just because
they disagree with you on many things. Instead, allow the sweet
aroma of the gospel to draw others to you so they want to
meet the One who saved you.

Today's Prayer

*Dear God, I don't want to play it safe and remain in my comfort
zone. I want to follow the example set by your Son and the saints
before me and break through barriers of prejudice, bias, and
favoritism. Today give me the strength and courage to relate to all
people, especially those outside my little world, so that they might
know the grace-filled, loving acceptance of your heart. Amen.*

Today's Reflection on Living, Loving, Leading

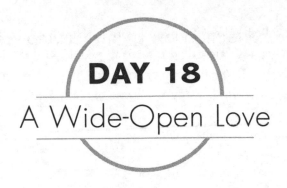

DAY 18
A Wide-Open Love

Today's Scripture

"But love your enemies, do good, and lend, hoping for nothing in return; and your reward will be great, and you will be sons of the Most High. For He is kind to the unthankful and evil. Therefore be merciful, just as your Father also is merciful."

LUKE 6:35–36 NKJV

Who we are and how we behave matters—it matters a great deal. Think about how the behavior and conduct of others either positively or negatively impacts you. Maybe you can recall a particular teacher at school who took the time to affirm you, giving you the courage to believe in yourself. Perhaps there was a pastor or mentor who went the extra mile to help you achieve your dream.

You may also have memories of someone who spoke or acted cruelly toward you, making you feel insignificant or useless. We should never underestimate the power we have over one another, especially the power of our leadership decisions over those who look to us for direction or support. It's not as though we have to be a perfect person to qualify in life—not at all—but we must be honest and teachable and live with authenticity and embrace others.

Jesus said, "'Love the Lord your God with all your passion and prayer and intelligence.' This is the most important, the first on any list. But there is a second to set alongside it: 'Love others as well as you love yourself.' These two commands are pegs; everything in God's Law and the Prophets hangs from them" (Matt. 22:37–40 MSG).

Today we are called to love the people who perhaps historically the Church has never reached. We are called to love all people with the love of Christ, because his Father loves all people, wants to bless all people, and wants to save all people. I never want to be one of those people whose attitude and body language convey condemnation, judgment, and condescension. I want to be someone with arms wide open, heart wide open, and mind wide open to loving the people around me.

There is nobody who doesn't deserve to walk into their local church and have others look them in the eye and understand that we are all in the same position. We are all sinful, flawed, selfish, imperfect people—saved only by the grace of God and the love of Christ and the power of the Holy Spirit.

Today's Thought

You and I are called to be dispensers of God's grace,
purveyors of love, both inside and outside the church.
It must be the tone of our lives.

Today's Prayer

*Dear Lord, I confess that it's not often easy for me to love my enemies.
Instead I allow my anger, frustration, resentment, and fear to
overtake my heart and cloud my judgment. Sometimes I say things
I don't mean to my enemies and I withhold love and forgiveness.
But this is not your way, Jesus. You loved everyone and mingled with
fishermen, tax collectors, and prostitutes. Today I want to love
my enemies and show them your kindness. Amen.*

Today's Reflection on Living, Loving, Leading

_____

_____

_____

DAY 19
We Are All God's Favorites

Today's Scripture

"A new commandment I give to you, that you love one
another; as I have loved you, that you also love one another.
By this all will know that you are My disciples,
if you have love for one another."

JOHN 13:34–35 NKJV

It seems to be human nature that we gravitate toward some people and not towards others. It may result from shared interests, common goals, or mutual respect and appreciation for one another's talents and abilities. We form a bond with them and consider them our "favorites."

We might have a favorite professional athlete or actor, a favorite employee or team member, even a favorite waiter or waitress. Consequently, we go out of our way to support their team, see their movie, assign them to important tasks, and sit in their section. We want to show them special favor and reward them for the bond we share.

However, God has no favorites, shows no partiality, and values no individual, group, or nation over another. This is wonderful news in theory but actually practicing this kind of impartial love can be quite challenging. While we want to love with the same all-inclusive embrace as our Savior, the reality is that we often fall short.

I'm convinced we have to keep our hearts open before God and ask him to deal with us, to keep us compassionate, merciful, loving, and aware of the grace we've been given. When we live out of the fullness of this awareness of God's grace in our lives, then we are compelled to show it and to share it with others. May we always be people who understand the power of the gospel and understand that God has no favorites because we're all his favorites. You're his favorite. I'm his favorite—just as the drunk or the street worker down the road is his favorite. We may like to think we're better than other people, but the truth is we are all loved by God with the same unconditional, unmerited, unimaginable love.

We are all his favorites.

Today's Thought

You can enjoy the abundant life filled with the loving presence of your Father and in turn share the unlimited resources of his love with everyone you encounter. With Jesus as our example, we who have been given grace are called to shine it into a dark world.

Today's Prayer

Dear Father God, thank you for the way you love me just as much as you love all your children. You want good things for me and know what's best even when I don't. Like a loving parent loves all their children in ways that are individualized and unique for each child, I want to love those around me with the same attention and compassion. Remind me that just as I am your favorite so are the people around me. We are all your precious children. Amen.

Today's Reflection on Living, Loving, Leading

_____

_____

_____

_____

_____

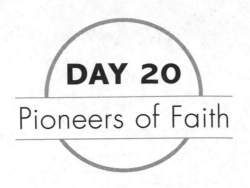

DAY 20
Pioneers of Faith

Today's Scripture

Looking unto Jesus, the author and finisher of our faith,
who for the joy that was set before Him endured the cross,
despising the shame, and has sat down at the
right hand of the throne of God.

HEBREWS 12:2 NKJV

Shortly after Bobbie and I started our church in a school in the north-west Hills District of Sydney, I realized I had to take risks if I wanted to engage and hold people's attention during my sermons. At the time I was twenty-nine years old, young and carefree, and one Sunday during my message—either out of excitement or desperation—I grabbed hold of one of two gymnastic ropes hanging from the school ceiling. I swung out over the congregation (which wasn't hard; they only went back a few rows), and there was a young man among the forty-five people there that day who found it so amusing.

The following week he went out and spoke to his friends, telling them, "You guys ought to come to my church—the pastor swings on a rope like a monkey!" The next week, he brought nine friends into the House of God, and all nine of them made commitments to Christ. The next week, they brought eleven more, and the following week, ten more. In three weeks he led thirty people to the saving grace of Jesus, and started a revival of passion in our little school hall. Little did he know that he was a pioneer.

When we think of the word *pioneer* today, we might immediately think of Amelia Earhart, Capt. James Cook, Christopher Columbus, Albert

Einstein, Steve Jobs, and countless others who have changed the face of history with their courageous and curious spirit. Their lives were dedicated to discovery and forward movement. Walt Disney, one of the twentieth century's most imaginative pioneers, once said of his growing empire, "Around here we don't look backwards for very long. We keep moving forward, opening up new doors and doing new things, because we're curious . . . and curiosity keeps leading us down new paths."

Pioneering takes courage, ingenuity, and a sense of adventure. With a pioneer spirit must come willingness to fail and falter, but with an unwavering belief in the long-term future vision. Pioneering doesn't come without its opposition, but the wide-open, spacious life we are seeking will undoubtedly require us to take some risks, step out of what is known, and count the cost of present comfort versus future reward. I believe it is God's will that we all have a pioneering spirit!

Today's Thought

When you walk with Jesus, you never stop being
a pioneer, blazing new trails as you explore uncharted
territories by faith.

Today's Prayer

Dear Jesus, it's easier for me to stick to familiar routes and
safe routines. But I know this is not the way you call me to follow
you and live my life. Today I ask for passion and boldness
to step out into the new territories you are opening before me.
Whether they're territories at home, work, church, school,
or my neighborhood, I pray you would ignite your
pioneering spirit within me. Amen.

Today's Reflection on Living, Loving, Leading

DAY 21
Small Seeds, Big Dreams

Today's Scripture

*"If you are faithful in little things, you will be faithful
in large ones. But if you are dishonest in little things,
you won't be honest with greater responsibilities."*

LUKE 16:10 NLT

I've been pioneering churches and pioneering in my life for over thirty years, and by God's grace I have never lost the pioneer spirit. When Bobbie and I moved to Australia in 1978, five years before we first began Hillsong Church, we pioneered a small church in a coastal area north of Sydney.

After a few months, it felt like the right time to hand that church on to another pastor, and shortly after that we were asked if we would consider taking on a church in Sydney's Southwest. This church was in a desperate state. The congregation was made up of three old ladies, the church itself met in an old building in a rough area, and their only asset was a dilapidated old minibus in the front driveway. When we arrived, I looked around to see a pulpit that was bigger than I was, and more plastic flowers throughout the sanctuary than I'd seen in my lifetime. Well, I removed the pulpit and the plastic flowers, and wouldn't you know...two of the three congregation members left! Yet, as we began to make some changes and ask God for wisdom, the church began to grow and new life sprung forth from it.

From there we began what is now known as Hillsong Church. I remember distinctly some of our early days of ministry—we were young and adventurous and desperate for God to work through us. Arriving early with a few volunteers, we would set up the little school hall where we met, and stay late to pack it down. We borrowed baseball caps to make up for forgotten offering containers, and the dusty broom cupboard was our preservice meeting room. I look back now and thank God that other people in our world caught our pioneering spirit.

I could never have imagined what God would grow with the seeds of my dreams for what Hillsong Church could become. The same is true for you. Whatever God has entrusted into your hand—your family, your career, your ministry—don't count it as insignificant and don't approach it with a lack of vision. In the eyes of God and with his leading, wisdom, favor, and provision—if you hold fast to that dream that he has placed in your heart and do it with a pioneering spirit, I believe you will see it come to pass.

Today's Thought

God delights in growing the small seeds of our faithful, pioneering actions into the trophies of his grace— accomplishments beyond our wildest dreams.

Today's Prayer

Dear God, it's hard for me to start new ventures and pioneer into unfamiliar areas sometimes. Instead I often give in to the temptation to focus on all the negatives and all the fears I have about what might happen. Today I want to be emboldened by your Spirit and step out into those wilderness areas that require me to be faithful in the small things. Because I know I can trust you always to be faithful in the big things. Amen.

Today's Reflection on Living, Loving, Leading

_____

_____

_____

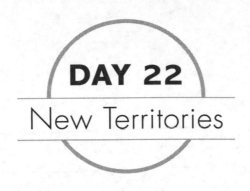

DAY 22
New Territories

Today's Scripture

*Philip went down to a city in Samaria and
proclaimed the Messiah there. When the crowds heard
Philip and saw the signs he performed, they all
paid close attention to what he said.*

Acts 8:5–6 NIV

As we live our lives, both collectively as the church and individually as followers of Jesus, we must maintain a raw-edged, risk-taking pioneering spirit in order to accomplish the dreams we have been given. Based on the model of loving leadership we see in Christ, a pioneer takes territory previously considered uninhabitable and realizes its potential.

Jesus always saw below the surface of people and knew what was in their hearts. He blazed a trail beyond human prejudices, biases, and stereotypes, and he calls his followers to do the same. He didn't follow the bandwagon and play it safe, sticking to familiar roads and traditional routes. Instead he boldly explored the wilderness of the human heart and the need we all have for a Savior.

We see this same pioneering spirit when Philip takes the gospel message to Samaria, a place looked down upon by the Jews, because the region was inhabited not only by Gentiles but also by Jewish people who had mixed with Gentiles. These people were seen as having compromised their heritage and were consequently viewed as outsiders, inferiors.

And yet there was Philip heading off to this undesirable area to be a pioneer of grace. Suddenly what had been viewed as uninhabitable and unreachable became a vital part of God's kingdom. In fact, as the gospel spread among the Gentiles, it was no longer only the Jews who were chosen by God. Because of what Christ did for us on the cross, everyone—you and I included—can be part of the family of God.

We still have so many people to touch with God's love in our lives today—territories inhabited by outsiders and looked down upon by so many others. Whether it's someone you know a few doors down who dresses differently and practices another faith, or the homeless teen asking for change on the corner, outsiders have never gone away. We may have mapped our planet many times over, but we still have new territories of faith to explore. And Jesus still calls us to be his pioneers.

Today's Thought

Pioneers of faith push through their fears of what others may think and the status quo of peer pressure so they can reach outsiders with the love of Christ.

Today's Prayer

Dear God, in today's world I'm sometimes afraid of people who look, act, and believe differently than I do. It's tempting to either criticize them or to dismiss and ignore them. But Jesus embraced outsiders, and I want to love the outsiders in my life with the same compassion, love, and concern he demonstrated. Today give me strength to push beyond my fears and the stereotypes of popular culture. Help me to see the humanity in all my brothers and sisters. Amen.

Today's Reflection on Living, Loving, Leading

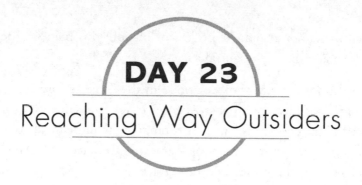

DAY 23
Reaching Way Outsiders

Today's Scripture

*For God gave us a spirit not of fear but of power
and love and self-control.*

2 TIMOTHY 1:7 ESV

Jesus consistently sought out people on the fringe of society, the individuals others dismissed. He talked to foreigners, women with bad reputations, men with deadly diseases, and children who wanted his attention. He refused to play the power games of the religious leaders of his day, leaving them frustrated and angry.

In Acts we see that his first disciples followed the same pattern. It was probably uncomfortable, inconvenient, and uncertain, but they obeyed the Lord's command to share the gospel of grace with all people, not just their Jewish neighbors. Christ destroyed the barriers of exclusion and the walls of elitism that many self-righteous Jews had constructed for themselves, and now his followers pioneered the wide-open territory left in his wake.

As evidence, consider that the first three individuals outside of Jerusalem whose lives were transformed by the gospel were not only outsiders but *way* outsiders—the least likely to be approached by Jews and to receive the good news of grace. The first was a sorcerer, a wizard named Simon who confounded people with his magic tricks.

The second one (in Acts 8) was an Ethiopian eunuch. He was not only African, from a different county and culture, but he had been castrated, most likely to serve as a servant to the women, probably wives and concubines, of a rich man's household. Regardless of his job, this man was definitely part of a small minority of outsiders.

And the third was Saul, who's described in the Bible as "breathing threats and murder" against Christians (Acts 9:1). Yet Saul, this assassin of the Christian faith, ended up having a dramatic encounter with God while traveling on the road to the city of Damascus. Blinded by the encounter, he soon realized the power of God's grace and became a new man. He went from being the angry assailant Saul to being the humble yet powerful apostle Paul.

So a former wizard, a eunuch, and a hit man—how's that for an encouraging front row in church? Sounds more like the setup for some kind of joke! Clearly, the gospel is for everyone, not just Jewish religious leaders or the wealthy or successful. All backgrounds, all situations, all ethnicities are welcome in God's family.

Today's Thought

Just as Philip dared to step into unknown territory to reach
those who were way outside his familiarity, we are God's
pioneers, called to go beyond our comfort zones
as we advance his kingdom.

Today's Prayer

Dear Lord Jesus, you and your disciples make it look so easy to love people who were on the fringes of society. But I find it so hard to reach out and help those people I don't like or don't understand. Whether it's a homeless person, a person of another faith, or a wealthy celebrity, I need to reserve judgment and simply accept them and love them as you would. We all need you in our lives— your forgiveness, grace, and power. Amen.

Today's Reflection on Living, Loving, Leading

_____

_____

_____

_____

_____

_____

_____

_____

_____

_____

_____

_____

_____

_____

_____

_____

_____

_____

_____

_____

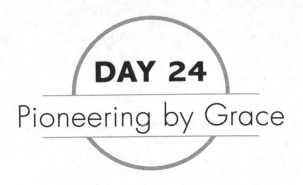

DAY 24
Pioneering by Grace

Today's Scripture

*Each of you should use whatever gift you have received to serve others,
as faithful stewards of God's grace in its various forms.*

1 PETER 4:10 NIV

Pioneering by grace is in the DNA of Hillsong Church. In 1977 my parents, who were then in their midfifties, moved from New Zealand to Sydney, Australia. They went to the eastern suburbs and found a little hall in Double Bay, where they started a church they called Eastern Suburbs Christian Life Centre.

It was many years later, in 1999, when Bobbie and I were given the opportunity to do something that for us at that time was a bold and innovative step. We were asked to take on the leadership of my parents' inner-city church in addition to Hillsong, the church we were already pastoring in the northwest of Sydney. Although today there are countless models of incredible multisite churches, back in 1999 it was totally new territory, and we had no role models to look to for guidance. We were pioneers.

Sixteen years on, our City Campus is a thriving and integral part of Hillsong Church. Along the way we have learned a great deal about multisite expansion and global church planting, as Hillsong has spread to some of the world's most influential cities: New York, London, Paris, and Los Angeles to name a few. I am not called to plant churches everywhere, but where we do, my hope and prayer is that we can build significant churches whose impact for the Cause of Christ spreads far beyond their own walls and welcomes everyone.

From the very beginning, we've always endeavored to be a pioneering church, not always having to do new things, but finding God doing fresh things as we've worked to hear his voice and follow his leading. It hasn't always been the easy road—sometimes it's been the costly one—but pioneering in the will of God has ultimately brought about great eternal fruit and reward.

Thirty years ago, with seventy people in our first service in a school hall in the suburbs of Sydney, we would have laughed at the idea of being influential. We haven't tried to be pioneers for the sake of recognition or novelty or fame. Over many years we have simply endeavored to build Christ's church and see people connect with Jesus, be discipled in his truth, and grow in God's purposes for their lives. I believe this is what it means to lead a big life: pioneering by following Christ's example.

Today's Thought

Pioneering by grace will always accomplish more—through the power of God—than our own efforts.

Today's Prayer

Dear Heavenly Father, today I thank you for the ways you have surprised me through your grace. When I look back on my life, I see so many moments when you provided exactly what I needed when I needed it. You always exceed what I'm able to imagine and accomplish so much more than anything I can do on my own. Empower me, God, to keep stepping into those places where my faith is stretched and my eyes are opened to your kingdom. Amen.

Today's Reflection on Living, Loving, Leading

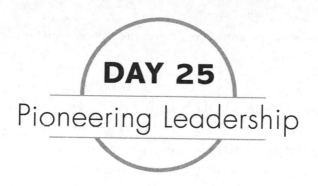

DAY 25

Pioneering Leadership

Today's Scripture

"For with God nothing will be impossible."

LUKE 1:37 NKJV

If you want to follow Jesus, to walk with him closely and experience the power of his love, then you must be a pioneer, a passionate leader in the exploration of the uncharted wilderness of your spacious life. Now you may not think of yourself as a leader, let alone a pioneer, based on the way our world and culture defines them. But if you follow Jesus, then you are a pioneering leader. If you have the Holy Spirit living in you, then God has anointed you as a leader in his revolution to free every human being from the slavery of sin.

We are each called to lead our lives in a way pleasing to God, in a manner that fulfills our divine potential, whether we're called to hold earthly positions of authority or not. Whether you are the leader of a global company, the leader of a Bible study at church, or simply a leader in your home with your children—you are a pioneer in your present territory!

If we ever lose that pioneering spirit, I wonder what enormous surprise we will never know we missed out on this side of eternity. What is it that is in your hand right now that requires courage, tenacity, maybe a bit of risk, and the spirit of a pioneer? What big discovery might be waiting right around the corner? Where are you continuing to search for God's guidance as you apply your talents and steward the resources you've been given?

No matter where you find yourself in life right now, it's not too late. Praise God, we have that same opportunity in our lives today, to believe God and to see new opportunities for growth, new possibilities for fulfilling our potential.

The big life we long to live can so often be hijacked by setbacks or stumbles, unexpected bumps in the road. But if we spend our time looking to or dwelling on the past, we may never meet the God appointment waiting for us in the future. Nothing is impossible for the One who has called you, sent you, and promises to do the journey with you.

Today's Thought

Pioneering leaders serve as stewards of all God has entrusted to them. They persevere through storms and trials and discover new ways to accomplish the dreams God has given them.

Today's Prayer

Dear Lord Jesus, I want to lead with the same strength, resilience, and courage I see in your example. You faced every encounter, every storm, and every trial by relying on your Father in heaven. Today remind me to lead with a sense of surrender and to serve those I seek to lead. Amen.

Today's Reflection on Living, Loving, Leading

_____

_____

_____

_____

_____

_____

DAY 26
When Trouble Strikes

Today's Scripture

The Lord delights in those who fear him, who put
their hope in his unfailing love.

PSALM 147:11 NIV

I think in life, especially as people of faith, we believe for the best. But let's be honest: If you live long enough, we will all have those days when we hear the worst. It could be the call in the middle of the night—never good news—about the health of an aging parent or from the police who have just arrested your teenage child. It could be a conversation with your boss, one that you thought was going to be a regular appointment that suddenly turns into your job's termination. It could be a routine checkup revealing something more serious, or a knock at your door resulting in a court summons in your hand.

I always try to live with an expectation for the best, but it's true that we never know what our worst day will be, or when it will be. What we do know is this: life is seasonal. The Bible virtually promises us that "in this world, we will have trouble" (see John 16:33). No matter how big and spacious our lives may be, how successful, wealthy, educated, or smart we are, we all encounter detours on the path of life that leave us in the ditch, things that blindside us, events we could never anticipate, secrets exposed we could never imagine.

Throughout the ordeals in my own life—and I have certainly seen my share—I kept going only because I knew God was with me. I have had to rely on his power to face those situations that were personally and professionally beyond my imagination. From revelations about my father to attacks by the press, from betrayals by friends to health scares within my family, I have learned there's really only one place I can go in such pain-filled moments. During seasons when everything seems to go wrong and nothing right, I have been forced to recognize again and again that I can do nothing without my Heavenly Father. In fact, the more responsibilities and opportunities he has entrusted to me, the more I must depend on him to carry them out.

When your world crashes at your feet and you can't imagine how to pick up the pieces, God is still with you. Even when you're blinded by pain and don't understand the circumstances, he is still there. He has promised to never abandon or forsake you.

―――――○―――――

Today's Thought

Through life's inevitable storms, the only way to survive and experience peace is by depending on your loving Heavenly Father. He knows your pain and has not forgotten you. He is with you.

Today's Prayer

Dear God, today I pray you would restore my hope and allow me to trust you more deeply and completely with all areas of my life. When I face life's storms, I often pull away from you and feel disappointed that things aren't going the way I want. Forgive me for these lapses, Lord, and remind me of your presence with me in the midst of anything I may be facing. Amen.

Today's Reflection on Living, Loving, Leading

―――――――――――――――――――――――

―――――――――――――――――――――――

―――――――――――――――――――――――

DAY 27

No Detours

Today's Scripture

No temptation has overtaken you except what is common to mankind. And God is faithful; he will not let you be tempted beyond what you can bear. But when you are tempted, he will also provide a way out so that you can endure it.

1 Corinthians 10:13 NIV

When the worst happens to you and me, we don't have the option to snap our fingers and make it go away, but Jesus could have. And yet he chose not to take the easy way out. Instead he chose to suffer and die as an innocent man so that all people, who certainly deserve punishment for their sins, could be forgiven and live forever.

However, Jesus was also fully human and apparently wrestled with how to handle the difficult path ahead of him. We see this in the conversation he had with his disciples in Matthew 16. After his followers tell Jesus that some people believed him to be John the Baptist or Elijah or another ancestral prophet, Christ then asked them who they thought he was. Peter answered correctly—that Jesus was indeed the Messiah, God's Son sent to earth to save his people.

Since it's not time for Jesus to reveal his identity publicly, however, he told his disciples to keep quiet. But he also told them about the difficult path that lay ahead of him once he revealed himself as the Son of God. This painful vision of the future upset Peter so much he took his Master aside and basically said, "No! This can't happen to you! I don't want this to happen and will not allow it."

Jesus then responded to Peter's outburst with a very dramatic exclamation of his own: "Get behind me, Satan!" He called his beloved friend, and the man he had earlier called the rock upon which he would build his church, the worst thing I can think of—Satan! Instead of a gentle, kind response, Jesus pushed back and called Peter a "stumbling block" (Matt. 16:23), more mindful of earthly things than the ways of God.

That's quite an indictment! But a response that clearly reflects Jesus' humanity. I think he basically said, "Look, Peter, this is hard enough! Don't tempt me to use my divine power to avoid all the painful events that I have to endure. You're trying to plant ideas in my head about how to avoid suffering. You're trying to get me to limit my view of God's plan and focus only on my own comfort. But that's shortsighted. So knock it off!"

We face the same temptation but have to keep our eyes on Jesus. He didn't take a detour around the shadowed valley ahead. So we must follow him through it.

Today's Thought

Although Jesus could have used his power as God's Son to avoid human suffering, instead he chose to lay down his power and experience excruciating emotional and physical pain in order to rescue us from the slavery of sin. We must keep his example before us when we suffer through life's painful trials.

Today's Prayer

Dear Jesus, sometimes I overlook that you have faced every temptation that I face in this life without ever yielding and sinning. Your example reminds me today that I can still experience powerful emotions such as anger, fear, and disappointment without letting them overtake my choices. I pray you would provide strength when I'm tempted and allow me to take comfort in my suffering by remembering the suffering you faced and conquered. Amen.

Today's Reflection on Living, Loving Leading

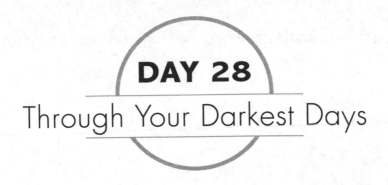

DAY 28
Through Your Darkest Days

Today's Scripture

*Surely goodness and mercy shall follow me all the days of my life;
and I will dwell in the house of the LORD forever.*

PSALM 23:6 NKJV

Whenever the path grows difficult for us, whenever we enter the valley of the shadow and feel as if the worst has happened, it is easy to struggle with being shortsighted and earthly minded. Just as Jesus called out Peter as being of the devil for tempting him to take an easy way out, I believe such thoughts originate from the same place of fear. We can't imagine how we'll get through such a painful ordeal, so we want to take the first way out we see. We don't want to have to suffer, uncertain of when—or if—we will come out the other side.

However, the example set by Jesus makes it clear there is no easy way out. We must confront the unthinkable and somehow walk the difficult path before us one step at a time. Whenever I think about the darkest valleys through which I've passed, I recognize that God never abandoned me. As painful as those times were—and sometimes still are—God promised to remain by my side throughout those dark valleys and desperate days. As a result, I've learned that facing the truth, no matter how painful, forces me to trust him at a deeper level than ever before.

He is there by your side as well. And without knowing the terrible events, painful disappointments, or even horrific abuse you may have endured, I firmly believe God is always there for us. Each of us must cling to our own revelation of Jesus whenever bleak days try to obscure our faithful path.

When we walk through the valley of the shadow, when we turn a corner and glimpse a difficult path filled with pain and heartache ahead, we can only go forward.

And in order to take the next step forward and then the next, we must lean on God and keep our eyes on Jesus. He has promised never to leave us or forsake us and will guide us through our darkest days. Even in the valley of the shadow, we can take comfort knowing God is still with us, still on our side, and still providing all we need to move forward.

Today's Thought

No matter how painful life becomes, cling to the promise that God will see you through your dark valleys.

Today's Prayer

Dear God, there are certainly plenty of painful realities in life today: relationships, finances, work stress, health concerns. In addition to the circumstances I'm facing, I'm also hurting for what my family, friends, and loved ones are suffering. Today I pray you would remind me of your power and provide me with your peace. I know when I rely on you, I can face anything, no matter how painful or disruptive it may be. Amen.

Today's Reflection on Living, Loving, Leading

_____

_____

_____

_____

_____

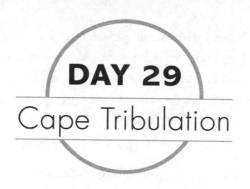

DAY 29
Cape Tribulation

Today's Scripture

To everything there is a season, a time for every purpose under heaven.

ECCLESIASTES 3:1 NKJV

Whenever I think about the way life can suddenly tilt into a crisis, I recall one of the great heroes of Australia, Capt. James Cook. Now there was a pioneer! In 1770 he sailed into Botany Bay, one of three harbors that form the backdrop of what is now the city of Sydney, along the east coast of Australia's mainland. He is generally considered the person who discovered Australia, though unfortunately he discovered it the hard way. No one told Captain Cook about the Great Barrier Reef, a twelve-hundred-mile shelf of beautiful but jagged coral and one of the world's great wonders. And as you might suspect, jagged coral and his old wooden ship, the *Endeavour,* didn't get along very well. So Captain Cook got caught on the reef in a perilous situation and his ship began to sink.

If not for the quick thinking of his resourceful crew, who began to throw objects overboard to lighten their weight, the *Endeavour* would have fallen into a watery grave. But crew members threw over everything they could get their hands on—ballasts, tools, jars of olives, bags of grain, even their cannons. They tossed all sorts of things overboard in order to survive. Eventually, their ship became light enough to float above the reef and continue to sail. The spot where they got stuck, however, has become rather famous. And guess what it's called? Cape Tribulation!

We all have our Cape Tribulations. Scripture even tells us that such trials are inevitable. Notice in the verse above (Ecc. 3:1) that it says there's a season for *everything* and a time for *every purpose*, even ones we don't like or want to face. As much as we may not like it or understand it, *everything* means all the painful, unexpected, disappointing, frightening, challenging moments as well as all the joyful, predictable, exciting, reassuring, and comfortable ones.

Life always includes times of pain, of mourning and grieving, of suffering and healing, and of fighting and reconciling. In order to get through life's storms, I'm convinced that we, like Capt. Cook, must let go of the burdens and excess baggage we're carrying when we hit our own Cape Tribulations. God can lift us above the riptides of life, but we must be willing to ask for his help, relinquishing our own attempts at control.

———————○———————

Today's Thought

The only way you can survive the inevitable tribulations
of life is by relying on God to guide you through them
and into safer waters.

Today's Prayer

*Dear Father, today I need your comfort, care, and guidance in
my life. Sometimes the losses of my life overwhelm me and I'm not
sure how I can keep going. But I know the only way to get back up
and stay on my feet when life knocks me down is to rely on you.
There are many things in life I don't understand—cancer, divorce,
abuse, and many more. But I trust you can redeem even my darkest
circumstances by shining your light of hope and love. Amen.*

Today's Reflection on Living, Loving, Leading

_____

_____

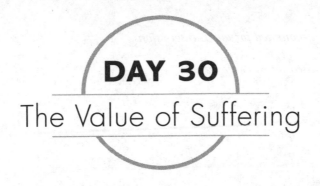

DAY 30
The Value of Suffering

Today's Scripture

*And the God of all grace, who called you to his eternal glory
in Christ, after you have suffered a little while, will himself
restore you and make you strong, firm and steadfast.*

1 PETER 5:10 NIV

Life is sometimes a difficult path, but it keeps going—and so must we. The greater problem occurs when we get stuck in our pain, when we can't seem to find the strength to get back on our feet and continue our journey. If we stop just because we're in pain and can't imagine how to continue, then we will miss out on what God wants to do in our lives.

I don't believe that suffering itself is from God, but I believe he uses our suffering—because with him, nothing is wasted. With Christ as our model for living, loving, and leading, we see that he suffered beyond what we can imagine so that we can enjoy the reality of eternal life:

He is despised and rejected by men,

a Man of sorrows and acquainted with grief.

And we hid, as it were, our faces from Him;

He was despised, and we did not esteem Him.

Surely He has borne our griefs

And carried our sorrows; yet we esteemed Him stricken,

Smitten by God, and afflicted.

But He was wounded for our transgressions,

He was bruised for our iniquities;

the chastisement for our peace was upon Him,

And by His stripes we are healed. (Isaiah 53:3–5)

We have a Savior who not only knows what it means to suffer but who willingly gave himself as a sacrifice in our place. He loved us enough to take more than a bullet for us—he took the cross. And he defeated sin and death so that we can have grace and joy and hope. Because Christ rose from the dead, we can endure the trials that come our way on life's difficult path.

Even when paralyzed by pain, we must find the faith to stand and take that next step. Even when it feels unbearable and our fears threaten to consume us, we must believe that God can somehow bring us through this time and restore our wellbeing. When we follow Jesus' example, then we know that pain cannot be avoided—but it can be used to make us more like him.

―――――――○―――――――

Today's Thought

Our suffering has value because it transforms us into being
more like Jesus, sacrificing our own comfort and convenience
for the benefit of others.

Today's Prayer

*Dear Jesus, help me to see the suffering in my life as a way to
draw closer to you. Use the pain in my life to give me a greater and
deeper compassion for the sufferings of other people around me.
Following your example, Lord, today I ask that you would help
me to take my eyes off my own troubles and instead seek to
comfort and serve someone else. Amen.*

Today's Reflection on Living, Loving, Leading

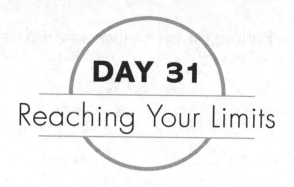

DAY 31
Reaching Your Limits

Today's Scripture

For I am persuaded that neither death nor life, nor angels nor principalities nor powers, nor things present nor things to come, nor height nor depth, nor any other created thing, shall be able to separate us from the love of God which is in Christ Jesus our Lord.

ROMANS 8:38–39 NKJV

I learned my own Cape Tribulation lesson, about letting go of the heavy weights bearing down on me, the hard way. Although I had handled revelations about my dad as best I could, relying on the power of God's Spirit to give me the courage, strength, and stamina to keep going, the ongoing pain took its toll. When my father passed away in 2004, I grieved for the dad I had known as well as the secret realities of the man I never knew.

Even as our church was flourishing in Australia and exploding globally, I was internally imploding. Finally, after years of struggling, I reached a point where the cumulative impact of all the stress, strife, and struggle became too much for me. My ship was sinking, weighed down by excess baggage and other issues of life, and I found myself shattered on a great reef of jagged pain, fear, and sorrow.

Then one day something collapsed within me. It was as if all the emotional strength in my tank had suddenly been drained. My doctor told me I had experienced an extreme panic attack, and eventually, I was diagnosed with Post-traumatic Stress Disorder (PTSD). The diagnosis made sense from a logical, clinical perspective, and in some ways I was relieved because suddenly I had a label for what I had been experiencing. Yet in some ways I was very shocked. Surely the doctors weren't talking about me!

While I always tried to be the one others could lean on for support, I had to come to terms with the fact that I wasn't invincible. Although my God is all-powerful, I am not. My body, mind, and spirit have limits.

By the grace of God, I bounced back quickly. Since my diagnosis, I have never had another panic attack and expect I never will. This bump in the road was unexpected, but with the help of my family, trusted counsel, and the peace of God, it didn't sink my ship.

Despite how painful your circumstances may be, no matter how difficult life's path may seem, you will not be destroyed. God meets you where you reach your limits. I believe life is all about choices, and we can choose to cooperate with the words of death and sickness spoken over our lives, or we can choose to rise above them. The anguish you feel is real, but there's something more powerful, more potent, more all-encompassing than any loss, crisis, or trauma we can encounter: the love of God through the power of his Son, Jesus Christ.

Today's Thought

No matter how difficult life's path, nothing can separate you from the love of God.

Today's Prayer

Dear Father God, I thank you for all the ways you sustain me through the various trials and tribulations of my life. I am so grateful that I can take refuge in you and experience peace that passes all understanding. I pray you would continue to protect and deliver me through the stormy seas I encounter. Amen.

Today's Reflection on Living, Loving, Leading

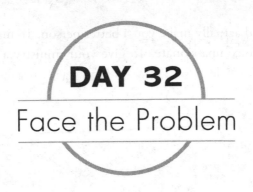

DAY 32
Face the Problem

Today's Scripture

He who dwells in the secret place of the Most High shall abide under the shadow of the Almighty.

PSALM 91:1 NKJV

When our kids were small, like many young families we opted for road trips instead of costly flights. These lengthy journeys in the car undoubtedly rang with the familiar question from the backseat: "Are we there yet?" My kids recall my response with sarcastic humor now, but my consistent answer would always be "No...we have miles and miles to go!" There was no watering down the long road ahead, and my honest response was in a considered effort to toughen them up for the journey.

Our trials are similar. While nothing on earth can separate us from God's presence, in order to recover, heal, and grow stronger, we must understand the process of pain has no shortcuts. While we wish it would go away tomorrow, most burdens don't just disappear the next morning. It's clear in the Bible that suffering and struggles are an ongoing process, not a onetime event or moment.

When I think about my own experiences, I often want to progress out of my challenges without having to embrace the process. However, we must all realize that pain cannot be neatly compartmentalized and boxed away on a shelf. The painful events we suffer bleed into our lives every day if we ignore them.

We often feel as if we can't see any good purpose in the trials of life whatsoever, but it's amazing how God can use anything and everything to take you forward and actually make you a better person. To make you stronger, wiser, and more compassionate. To give your ministry a bit more depth, your business a new lease on life, your family a second chance at affection and understanding. To force you into his arms for a closer, more intimate relationship.

In Scripture there are many examples to describe what happens when we don't wait on God's timing and embrace the process of painful circumstances. When we procrastinate and avoid the hard choices and difficult actions necessary to move through our pain, it usually results in calamity. Denial only compounds the pain and causes it to grow and fester like an infection in your body.

Don't delay what should be addressed at the beginning of the process in hopes that you can avoid it or somehow minimize your suffering. As excruciating as it feels at the time, doing the right thing and being obedient to God allows you to move through the process faster and more aware of what is to come.

Today's Thought

If you try to bypass the process of pain during life's trials, you may also miss out on what God has for you in the midst of them.

Today's Prayer

Dear God, forgive me for frequently trying to avoid life's pain so I can focus only on my own pleasure, comfort, and convenience. Thank you for reminding me of the ways you can comfort and console me in the midst of painful circumstances, and how such times can bring us closer. Today I don't want to miss out on what you have for me because I'm afraid of hurting. Help me to face my problems and know that you will lead me through them. Amen.

Today's Reflection on Living, Loving, Leading

DAY 33
Soul Supporter

Today's Scripture

*I cry out to the LORD with my voice; with my voice to the
LORD I make my supplication. I pour out my complaint
before Him; I declare before Him my trouble.*

PSALM 142:1–2 NKJV

Embracing the process of pain does not mean wallowing in self-pity or relying on your own efforts to get you through your suffering. The first thing you must do is accept the fact that we all need support. When you're in the midst of a trial filled with turmoil and trauma, then you need the comfort of others, you need support, and you need God.

While the Bible contains many examples of how difficult life can be amidst the process of pain, perhaps there's no better, more concentrated example of this truth than what we find throughout the Psalms. The Psalms are a collection of poems and song lyrics, many of them written by David, the shepherd boy who became king of Israel. Many of David's beautiful words reflect the joy and sheer wonder he experienced in his relationship with God. But many of them also reflect his anger, his pain, his grief, and his fear.

In one of his rawest expressions, Psalm 142, David makes it clear that sometimes we must voice our pain before the Lord. Obviously, God already knows what we're going through and how we feel so such expression is for our benefit, not God's. From there, David launches into a bit of a laundry list about why he's feeling so down. Basically, he reveals just how low he feels with a sense that everyone's out to get him, setting snares for him, ignoring his pain, and not acknowledging his need for comfort. Such emotions can be common to us all: "Nobody cares about me." "That person is out to get me." "Why isn't anyone helping me?" "Woe is me!"

But then David concludes the Psalm by reminding himself of what he knows to be true: "Lord, you are my refuge!" (see Ps. 142:5). In fact, this theme and this very phrase occurs in many other Psalms, including 18, 46, 62, and 91. We must cry out to God, letting him know how overwhelmed we are with pain, with grief, with anger.

I can't tell you how many times I've felt overwhelmed by my silent pain. Yet even when I wasn't sure I could handle it, I knew God could handle my pain. So like David, I cried out to him and reminded myself of what I knew to be true, even if I didn't particularly feel it in that moment.

Today's Thought

God will *always* be your soul supporter…especially on your worst days.

Today's Prayer

Dear Lord, I often suppress my pain and fearful emotions from you because I'm afraid of suffering, afraid my grief and hurt will swallow me. But I know you can handle anything I feel and understand and accept my cries. Today I want to bring my heartaches before you so that I can experience your divine peace and healing. Today I will take comfort from knowing you are still in charge of my life. Amen.

Today's Reflection on Living, Loving, Leading

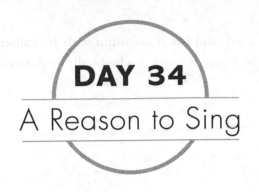

DAY 34
A Reason to Sing

Today's Scripture

*For I consider that the sufferings of this present time
are not worth comparing with the glory that
is to be revealed to us.*

ROMANS 8:18 ESV

While my sons were in high school, they met a young man named Matt, or "Stealth," as all his mates called him. At a young age, Stealth had been adopted into a wonderful family but lost his mum to cancer when he was only seventeen. A few years later, his father passed away as well, leaving Stealth and his siblings as orphans. He needed family, and it was our privilege to bring him into our world.

Stealth lived out his university days alongside my son Joel, and he was a fixture in our church—where he met Jill, a Hillsong College student from the United States. An incredibly talented young lady, Jill served on our worship team as a leader and songwriter. Their romance developed quickly, until they were eventually married; a couple of years later they were thrilled to be expecting their first child.

Max Kingston McCloghry was born at just twenty-three weeks gestation and went to be with Jesus on the same day. The grief that Stealth had already experienced in his young life culminated that night in February as he and Jill wept over the son they had longed for and loved, only to be disappointed by such an unfair and unexplainable tragedy. Our family wept with them.

Only days after Baby Max's funeral, Brooke Ligertwood was finishing the lyrics to a new song, and her relationship with Jill caused her to ask her friend—who was going through undoubtedly her darkest hour—if she would consider leading worship alongside her that night, only weeks after her loss. As Jill bravely took to the platform that evening, the sense of God's presence was so tangible as she boldly declared:

All of my life, in every season,

You are still God.

I have a reason to sing, I have a reason to worship.

"Desert Song," Hillsong Music, 2008

Grief is a hard road, and one that is not to be diminished. Yet, many years on, still walking out their journey of healing (and being a blessing to many others who are walking theirs), Jill and Matt are raising two beautiful children, gifts from God, and living a big, wide-open life in New York City. Through the choices of people whose hearts were steadfast and in love with Jesus, and because of the unending grace of an Almighty God, what began as a prison of pain has become a prism of praise.

Today's Thought

Even during your greatest losses, you still have a reason to sing, a reason to worship. God remains ever present through each and every season, the good and the bad, that you experience.

Today's Prayer

Dear God, it's hard to see your hand at work during my darkest times. In those moments of crisis and loss, nothing seems to make sense, and my grief and sadness overwhelm me. Even then— especially in those moments—I pray you would meet me in my distress and comfort me. Today, Lord, hold me close and help me to give you my pain and suffering. Amen.

Today's Reflection on Living, Loving, Leading

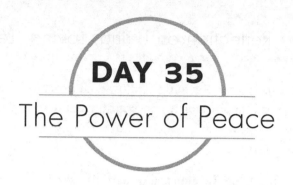

DAY 35
The Power of Peace

Today's Scripture

And the peace of God, which passeth all understanding,
shall keep your hearts and minds through Christ Jesus.

PHILIPPIANS 4:7 KJV

No matter who you are, or how many years you've been a Christian, everyone will come up against challenges and trials at times. But in these times you discover that the strength of your spirit and the health of your soul comes from God. Such setbacks do take a toll, and we look to both God and people for comfort, but the Bible tells us not to let the troubles of this world devastate you. "A healthy spirit conquers adversity, but what can you do when the spirit is crushed" (Prov. 18:14 MSG).

Sometimes I fear we get in the way of the supernatural healing God wants to give us in the midst of our pain. If I had fixed my thoughts only on what my dad did and all the terrible repercussions, then I would have indeed become paralyzed with sorrow, anger, and bitterness. So I had to keep my perspective focused on Christ. *What you focus on in life determines whether or not you will experience peace in your heart.* The Bible gives us clear instructions about finding and living in a place of peace, as well as what takes away our peace.

Anxiety and worry work in opposition to inner peace. When you are worried or anxious about something, even something that must be faced and embraced as a process, you leave little room for God's peace. As I have discovered, worrying is a genuine health hazard. The Bible tells us, "Anxiety in the heart of man causes depression, but a good word makes it glad"

(Prov. 12:25) or as the New Living Translation renders it, "Worry weighs a person down; an encouraging word cheers a person up."

Peace will flow like a river if you don't allow your heart to harden and form a dam. Worrying is about trusting in your own ability and not resting in the faith of God's power and goodness. You simply have to focus on the present moving forward.

If you want to live a big, spacious, abundant life like Jesus, especially when life gets difficult, then make the daily decision to believe God at his Word. Ask God to help you be patient as you move through the process of pain and wait for his promises over your life to be fulfilled. Ask him to fill you with hope and trust, believing him to be a good God who desires good things for your life.

Today's Thought

Commit to going the distance with God, allowing his grace to carry you, empower you, and sustain you when you're overwhelmed and can't imagine how you'll keep going.

Today's Prayer

Dear Jesus, I know you suffered so much more than I have or will. You faced injustice, betrayal, hatred, prejudice, and were murdered by those people you came to save. Your suffering reminds me that I can keep going, trusting you to carry me through the trials. Today I will focus on the ways your grace sustains me in the midst of difficult times. Amen.

Today's Reflection on Living, Loving, Leading

_____

_____

_____

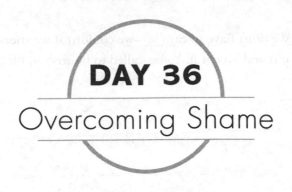

DAY 36
Overcoming Shame

Today's Scripture

*For if by the one man's offense death reigned through the one,
much more those who receive abundance of grace and
of the gift of righteousness will reign in life
through the One, Jesus Christ.*

ROMANS 5:17 NKJV

One of the greatest obstacles to enjoying the blessings God grants us is the heavy weight of shame. Sadly, many people don't understand the power of shame and what it's doing to them, the prison it keeps them in. Shame isolates us and weighs on us, burdening us with the past in ways that try to sabotage our glorious future. However, the good news is that through salvation in Jesus Christ, we have freedom from shame.

You see, everyone has a past. You're not on your own with shame over past mistakes and failures. Everyone has things they want to forget, things they want to leave behind, things that haunt them with sleepless nights. So often, we allow our past to define our frame of mind, the way we feel and the way we think.

Whether your past indiscretions were years ago or as recent as last night, there is power over the bondage that sin wraps around you. The Bible tells us that the wages of sin is death (see Rom. 6:23). If you think about that for a moment, you realize that what we earn when we sin is our own destruction. We usually think about earning wages for a paycheck, but when we sin we earn the wages of death.

Grace, on the other hand, grants us a gift—the precious gift of righteousness before God. We don't have to earn it—we couldn't if we tried—so we only have to ask for it and accept it. You're called to flourish in life, to enjoy that wide-open, free, and abundant life we have through Christ. Here's how the Old Testament describes this gift: "The righteous shall flourish like a palm tree." It goes on, "He shall grow like a cedar in Lebanon. Those who are planted in the house of the Lord shall flourish in the courts of our God" (Ps. 92:12–13).

If you're living under the weight of guilt, of shame, of condemnation, you're not flourishing. Instead of having dominion, you're being dominated—dominated by things that have no power or value in your life whatsoever. But you don't have to live this way. While I'm not saying you should ever take your past sins lightly, you must never lose sight of the real hope you have in Christ. Your focus should be on following Jesus, not on looking over your shoulder and regretting what you can't change. Shame is a prison, but the door to your cell is open.

Jesus calls you to follow him in the freedom of grace.

Today's Thought

Shame over your past sins will bind you and prevent you from enjoying the full, abundant life God has for you if you let it. Defeat shame by focusing on the power of grace you have through the love of Christ.

Today's Prayer

Dear Father, today I pray for protection from the enemy and ask you to bind the shame that he often uses to ensnare me. Please give me clarity and wisdom so I can discern between an awareness and conviction about my sins, knowing your grace dispels shame like the light banishes the darkness. I belong to you, God, and my relationship with you is secure because of what Jesus has already done. There is no room for shame in my big, spacious, abundant life. Amen.

Today's Reflection on Living, Loving, Leading

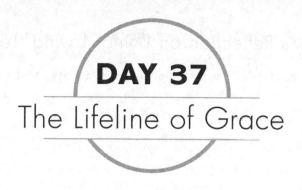

DAY 37
The Lifeline of Grace

Today's Scripture

The way of life winds upward for the wise.

PROVERBS 15:24 NKJV

If a building is condemned, that means it's unfit for use. It's disqualified. It's only good for being pulled down. That's how a lot of people live their lives. They live feeling condemned, unfit when it comes to serving God, perhaps even when it comes to being in the house of God, when it comes to worship, when it comes to the grace of God. They feel unworthy, unforgivable, and even unlovable.

One of my favorite verses is the one above, from Proverbs 15:24. Sadly, rather than gaining wisdom from their mistakes and winding upward, some people go on a steep decline, a downward spiral. Because here's what happens: Sin leads to guilt, guilt leads to shame, and ultimately shame leads to condemnation. Condemnation leads to death.

Some people are saved but they're not free. They don't believe they deserve to be happy, to enjoy the spacious, joyful life God has for them. They feel as if they're disqualified. They're unfit for happiness. But it's not true! It's nothing more than the devil's lies.

Sin becomes guilt, which is something we feel, an emotion. However, shame is something you carry, a state of being. People will sometimes say, "Shame on you!" and try to throw it at you. They judge you, condemn you, and try to make you feel the harsh sting of their rejection.

Have you ever had shame put on you? Ever feel worse because of the way others treated you or looked at you after they knew what you had done? While sin is something we do, and emotions are something we feel, shame is on a different level. It's something you carry, a weight and a burden. You walk down the street with it and feel it pressing down on you. Ultimately, it's exactly the opposite of the blessing of God.

If we want to shake off shame, we must understand the full power of what Jesus Christ has done for us. If you carry shame, then you're not carrying what comes with the blessing of God. With the blessing of God, you have the full benefit of all that's in his name. There is no other name that provides salvation that liberates the captives, that forgives the condemnation of sin. If you feel like you're sliding down the shame slope, it's time to wise up and grab the lifeline of grace.

Today's Thought

No matter how you may feel sometimes, Christ has set you free
from the power of shame, condemnation, and death.

Today's Prayer

*Dear Lord, I want to learn and grow from my past mistakes
and failures. Give me wisdom and help my path to wind upward
rather than allowing my shame, fear, and self-contempt to overwhelm
me. Today I will claim the freedom I have in Christ and
will no longer allow condemnation to rule over me.
I praise you for setting me free! Amen.*

Today's Reflection on Living, Loving, Leading

_____

_____

_____

_____

DAY 38
Blue Skies

Today's Scripture

For all have sinned and fall short of the glory of God.

ROMANS 3:23 NKJV

So many people allow their actions to be poisoned by shame, and then it controls them. Shame robs you of the blessings God has for you, and it tries to rule you so that you won't experience the full force of Christ's love. Shame makes a difficult path even more treacherous and deadly.

If you allow other things to be put on you, if you allow other things to rob you and rule you and bind you, then unfortunately you're living far short of what God has got for you.

Sin belittles you. It makes you feel isolated and alone, ashamed of your failures and indiscretions in a way that makes you feel as if you're the only one struggling with sin. But as Scripture makes clear, all of us have sinned. You're not the only one who has messed up and needs God's grace.

If you dwell on your mistakes and imperfections, if you focus only on how you fall short of the glory of God, it means that sin makes you smaller. It diminishes you—your potential, your relationship with God, and your confidence. You can't walk around with boldness and confidence if you're walking around hanging your head with the heavy weight of shame.

When people live ruled by shame, it has a huge toxic effect. They live under the power of condemnation, like someone with a black cloud constantly hanging over them. In fact, *The Message* often describes condemnation as a black cloud, one that's always about to send a thunderbolt to punish you.

But this does not align with the truth of God's Word and the power of Christ's death and resurrection. We're told, "God so loved the world that He gave His only Begotten Son" (John 3:16). And we're also told exactly why he sent him: "God did not send His Son into the world to condemn the world, but that the world through Him might be saved" (John 3:17). So many people know well the first part of this verse, but the fullness of its power is actually revealed in the second. Your Father wanted to give you the freedom of a full and vibrant life; he wanted you to experience salvation and life in abundance.

So he sent Jesus.

Today's Thought

Fold up your fear and shame like an old umbrella.
You now live under the clear blue skies of God's grace—
not the black cloud of condemnation.

Today's Prayer

*Dear God, you have paid the ultimate price—your only Son—
so that I can be forgiven and be close to you. Thank you for loving
me so much that you want me to spend eternity with you as your
child. I rejoice that you have banished shame, condemnation,
and death from my life and have replaced them
with grace, joy, and life. Amen.*

Today's Reflection on Living, Loving, Leading

_____

_____

_____

_____

DAY 39
Unexpected Kindness

Today's Scripture

Fear not, for I am with you; be not dismayed, for I am your God; I will strengthen you, I will help you, I will uphold you with my righteous right hand.

ISAIAH 41:10 ESV

I know firsthand the way shame can ambush you from around the next corner. Back in 2002, Hillsong Church was known around the world because of our worship music, but in Australia most people had never heard of us. The average person on the street probably didn't know we existed.

However, we suddenly burst through the surface of mainstream culture in an unforgettable way. Like many countries, Australia's largest newspapers have their big editions on weekends, usually with a splashy magazine in the center of the paper. So one Saturday the newspaper with Australia's largest circulation came out with Bobbie and me on the cover of their weekend magazine. Nothing about it was flattering.

We were so humiliated and upset, so hurt. We had naively cooperated and posed for photos with the writer of the article several weeks earlier and had tried to be as transparent as possible. And now it had bitten us. Our words had been distorted, our motives questioned.

We were in Bondi Beach the same Saturday morning that the papers hit. I remember walking along the familiar boardwalk, a place we loved and where we previously felt at home, but now feeling so humiliated, so ashamed.

Eventually, we went into a café to have breakfast. Embarrassed and trying to keep a low profile, I ordered an orange juice when our waiter came. A couple minutes later he returned with the most amazing glass of OJ I've ever seen. Instead of just the normal juice glass, my drink had all these beautiful fruit garnishes all around the rim of this giant tumbler of fresh-squeezed orange juice. After setting it before me, our waiter looked at me and said, "You're a good guy."

His words, his kindness, and the unspoken reference he was making spoke to my soul. They broke the yoke of shame bearing down on me. I've never felt so grateful to a waiter in a restaurant before. It's amazing how God uses moments in our lives to communicate and assure us of his love. He wanted me to know that just because the paper had printed all these distortions and fabrications didn't mean that everyone believed it.

I refused to allow shame to rule me then, and I forbid shame from clinging to me now. I'm a free man because of the grace of Jesus Christ. I am loved by my Heavenly Father beyond measure.

And so are you.

Today's Thought

Despite our enemy's attempts to discourage us with shame,
God consistently reminds us of his loving presence and
unconditional mercy in our lives.

Today's Prayer

*Dear Lord, I know the enemy of my soul will do everything
possible to discourage me and derail my faith. But I know you
are stronger than anything he can throw at me and will protect
me from all his snares. Thank you for the ways you remind me of
your loving presence, especially during trials and times of distress.
Your kindness never ceases to amaze me. Today I praise you
for your unfailing love. Amen.*

Today's Reflection on Living, Loving, Leading

DAY 40
Time to Flourish

Today's Scripture

There is therefore now no condemnation to those who are in Christ Jesus, who do not walk according to the flesh, but according to the Spirit.

ROMANS 8:1 NKJV

We've got to learn how to live our lives as saved men and women. And that means freedom from sin, freedom from guilt, freedom from shame, freedom from condemnation. Remember, sin is something you do, guilt is something you feel, and shame is something you carry. And eventually the weight of shame overtakes you and then condemnation takes you out. Condemnation would have you believe that just like a condemned building, you too are unfit for use.

That's not the will of God for you at all. And we never reach a point where we don't need reminding. When our path becomes difficult, shame will attempt to hijack our route. Sometimes it's when life is going well and you're enjoying a major blessing from the Lord. The devil can't stand for you to enjoy God's goodness without trying to thwart you and smother you with shame.

You have to understand the victory that God gives you over shame. I believe you've got to learn how to walk tall in the good news of the gospel of our Lord, Jesus Christ. He gives you every reason to hold your head up and walk tall and refuse to allow shame to be put on you. Live free.

We don't have to throw off the shame that tries to lock us in a chokehold on our own. Christ has broken its power for us. Notice the distinction made

128

in Romans 8:1 (above). It doesn't say you won't have temptation, and it doesn't say that things won't try to rear their ugly heads at times. But there is no condemnation! It has no claim on you and your big, abundant life of freedom in Christ. God wants to break the power of shame over your life.

What about you? Can you believe that you have absolutely nothing to be ashamed of because of what Jesus has done for you? Or are you still condemning yourself? Maybe you believe that God has forgiven you. Maybe you accept that other people are willing to forgive you for the ways you've hurt them. But are you willing to let God's grace sink down into your bones?

The path of life has enough difficulties of its own without us making it harder than it has to be. Don't allow the enemy to taunt you with your past mistakes. God doesn't remember them, so why should you? Righteousness is your free gift. Live in it, soak it up, and flourish like a palm tree.

Today's Thought

You are forgiven and have everything you need to enjoy the free, wide-open, abundant life Jesus came to give to you.

Today's Prayer

Dear God, today I thank you that I live by faith and not by shame. I praise you for loving me and liberating me from the shackles of sin in my life. And most of all, I give you thanks for your Son. I belong to Jesus and he is with me always. I have everything I need to enjoy the fullness of the life you have given me. Amen.

Today's Reflection on Living, Loving, Leading

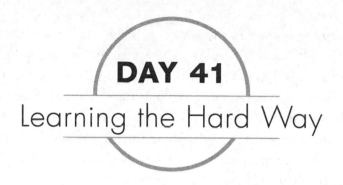

DAY 41

Learning the Hard Way

Today's Scripture

The fear of the LORD is the beginning of wisdom: and the knowledge of the holy is understanding.

PROVERBS 9:10 KJV

In the early days of Hillsong Church, I wrote a book titled *You Need More Money.* What was I thinking? I was young and eager, with little influence outside of our own local church, and I thought readers would be drawn to a provocative title. I may as well have painted a bull's-eye on my head, because critics took the title and labeled us "prosperity preachers" teaching a "prosperity gospel." I hate that term! There has only ever been one gospel, and one gospel alone—the gospel of Jesus Christ.

Needless to say, the media had a field day, rarely bothering to read the book itself. If they had, they would have realized my point: without money, it's hard (as a ministry, a business, a family) to fulfill the kingdom endeavors that are in your heart. Missionaries need money, churches need money, educating your children requires money. The book also outlines many of the perils that come with the love of money and how God is not interested in attitudes of greed, but rather in blessing us so that, in turn, we might use what we have to further his kingdom.

Looking back, I should have taken far more care so that the book couldn't have been taken out of context and lost its effectiveness. It is an unwise person who doesn't learn a lesson from such criticism. Even if facts were wrong or skewed, perceptions can teach us things and cause us to be better and do better—if we let them.

Developing the courage to live with conviction and accountability is the doorway to fulfillment in life, love, and leadership. In my experience, it is always worth the effort to work through hurt and disappointment, and see your less-than-ideal circumstances as opportunity for growth and learning, rather than becoming a victim. There are three ways to learn from our mistakes: the easy way, the hard way, and the tragic way. The easy way is learning from other people's mistakes. The hard way is learning from our own. And the tragic way is not learning from either.

Don't waste your mistakes by not learning from them—allow them to teach you, allow yourself to grow in them and become a better person because of them. And when your worst day becomes a long season, you can take courage from knowing that there will be faithful people who are ready and willing to make the journey alongside you every bumpy step of the way.

Today's Thought

Your biggest mistakes can often become your greatest teachers if you're willing to listen to your critics with a humble spirit.

Today's Prayer

Dear God, I often say I want to grow in wisdom but waver when it comes to paying the price. Help me to lean on you and trust your ways and not my own. Allow my faith to flourish as I constantly learn from my mistakes and the lessons you are teaching me. Amen.

Today's Reflection on Living, Loving, Leading

_____

_____

_____

_____

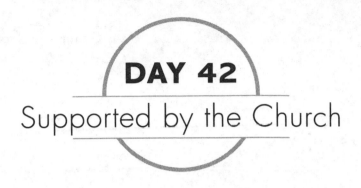

DAY 42
Supported by the Church

Today's Scripture

And let us consider how we may spur one another on toward love and good deeds, not giving up meeting together, as some are in the habit of doing, but encouraging one another— and all the more as you see the Day approaching.

HEBREWS 10:24–25 NIV

One of the great temptations, when life's path becomes difficult, is to isolate yourself. It is a natural instinct to try to pull back from your emotions and not feel the sharp pain caused by your crisis. If you're like me in such moments, you may also feel the need to retreat and become isolated. Even when you're around people, you can withdraw emotionally.

Going through a trial, a temptation, or turmoil makes you feel quite vulnerable, so it's natural to want to put up your walls and hide behind them. But that never helps the problem and it's little comfort. When you least feel like having fellowship with others is often when you need it the most. God understands the value of relationship, the value of the team. By nature, he exists as a trinity—a concept I just love. He is the God of the universe, and yet he still chooses to partner with us to see his plans and purposes worked out on the earth.

When you're struggling through a difficult part of your path, the best thing you can do is get into a great, positive, faith-filled environment. And this is where the local church can be so invaluable.

During the seasons of intense media scrutiny and criticism, the support Bobbie and our children and I personally received from our own local church and from many others was unparalleled. Attempts to discourage us and throw mud at us only caused people who knew differently through their own experience of Hillsong to rise up in courage and stand firm on what they believed—that Bobbie and I have always endeavored to live by the principles that we teach others.

We have always aspired to build a church that was youthful in spirit, generous at heart, faith filled in confession, loving in nature, and inclusive in expression. Sadly, I recognize that not every community has a healthy expression of the local church, and this is where we need to be planted in the Word of God—so we can speak to our own soul, claim victory, and rise up in Jesus' name. But remember, the perfect church doesn't exist, so don't underestimate the value of building healthy, God-glorifying relationships wherever your find yourself.

Today's Thought

The encouragement, prayers, and support of other believers
are an essential part of surviving life's trials.

Today's Prayer

*Dear Jesus, I usually feel so alone when circumstances change
and life becomes painful. Sometimes I withdraw from other people
and the help they offer—sometimes I even withdraw from you.
Forgive me for not sharing my burdens with you and trusting you
to carry them with me. And forgive me for not accepting the help of
others. Today I will share at least one of my struggles with a
trusted believer and ask them to pray for me. Amen.*

Today's Reflection on Living, Loving, Leading

DAY 43

A Multitude of Counselors

Today's Scripture

*Where there is no counsel, the people fall; but in the
multitude of counselors there is safety.*

PROVERBS 11:14 NKJV

Throughout the Psalms it's clear David understood the process of pain. But he also realized the incredible importance of allowing others to support him. After his prayer that God would release his soul from prison (Psalm 142), he declared, "the righteous shall surround me" (v. 7).

David knew that when you're feeling surrounded by accusation or by people who don't understand you or care about your suffering, that's when you need God's people the most. I encourage you to choose, during times of difficulty and discouragement and despite your natural inclination, to plant yourself in an environment where praise can take your focus off your problems and restore your gaze on an eternal perspective. Do all you can to get around people who can sit with you in your pain and not try to fix your problems or give you pat answers. People who will carry you with their faith when yours feels a bit weak and beaten up.

In the same way, it is unwise to trust your heart's pain with just anyone. You've got to gather trusted confidants, people you love and trust, people who know your heart and can handle your fragile state. Notice in the Scripture verse above (Prov. 11:14), it says a multitude of *counselors*, not a multitude of opinions. So don't trust just anyone—the neighbor on the corner, the lady in the checkout line, the guy at the gym, or the coworker at the office. Instead, focus on the people who share your faith.

It has amazed me in the past to see people lose their way when they allow their hairdresser, whose own world is a catastrophe, to become their counselor. Nothing against hairdressers, but the same can be said of unchurched colleagues and neighbors. Sharing your woes with people whose own lives don't line up with the will of God can lead to bad advice and poor choices. Look for the people in your life who love you and love God and clearly want what's best for you, with no agendas or strings attached.

***

Today's Thought

Choose your confidants carefully, selecting people who share
your faith and know your character.

Today's Prayer

*Dear God, thank you for the people you have placed in my life
who care about me and support me with their love, kindness, and
friendship. Help me not to take them for granted. And allow me to be
that same kind of supportive, loving friend to them. Give me
wisdom about who to trust with my heart. Amen.*

Today's Reflection on Living, Loving, Leading

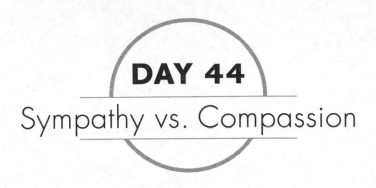

DAY 44
Sympathy vs. Compassion

Today's Scripture

"Then you will know the truth, and the truth will set you free."

JOHN 8:32 NIV

Everyone loves a little sympathy. In the Old Testament, one of the kings of Israel, King Ahab, sought counsel from four hundred prophets before he went into battle. All four hundred prophets were sympathetic to their ruler, and they told the king what he wanted to hear: that yes, the Lord would surely bring him victory. But there was one young prophet who chose to hear from the Lord, not bow to the power of intimidation.

In 1 Kings 22 we see that even the king himself recognized that he was simply searching for people who would sympathize with him and bring a good word that justified what he wanted to do. After calling all four hundred prophets together, "the King of Israel replied to Jehoshaphat, 'There is one more man who could consult the LORD for us, but I hate him. He never prophesies anything but trouble for me!'" (v. 8 NLT).

This story always makes me smile—the king outwardly confessing he would rather hear what he wants to hear, rather than the truth. Have you ever avoided someone because they were a truth teller and had things to say that you didn't want to hear? I have, and let me tell you, it certainly didn't help me then and it won't help you now.

When you're going through a rough patch, you want friends, colleagues, mentors, or pastors who have the guts to tell you the truth and to remind you of God's truth—not people who are simply trying to please you. People who will give you advice motivated by love and not judgment, condemnation, or manipulation.

My own experience has led me many times to receive counsel from people who are older than me or more mature in their faith and have come through their own challenges—people who have grown stronger from it and can offer you real support, wisdom, love, and assurance.

Not one time do we ever find Jesus being moved with sympathy; but every time he was moved with *compassion* something powerful was about to happen—a miracle was on its way. That's because sympathy identifies with the problem, but compassion gets up, looks up, and says, "I need to do something about this."

So when you are struggling on the difficult path, find someone who will look you in the eye, put their hands on your shoulders, and tell you the unvarnished truth, the truth of God's love, hope, healing, and power in your life.

Today's Thought

People who love God will tell you the truth even when it's painful and you don't want to hear it. You need these people in your life to overcome your blind spots.

Today's Prayer

*Dear Heavenly Father, I know I have blind spots in my life,
and I'm grateful for the strong believers you have given me to hold
me accountable and to help me grow. When I'm struggling with
difficult circumstances, I need to be reminded of the truth—
about who I am, about who you are, and about my purpose.
Thank you for those truth-tellers in my life, and may I
bless them in the same way. Amen.*

Today's Reflection on Living, Loving, Leading

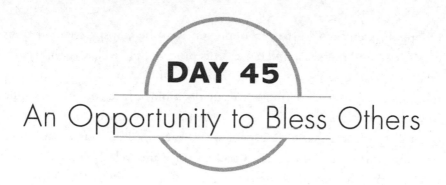

DAY 45

An Opportunity to Bless Others

Today's Scripture

Blessed be the God and Father of our Lord Jesus Christ,
the Father of mercies and God of all comfort, who comforts
us in all our affliction, so that we may be able to comfort
those who are in any affliction, with the comfort with
which we ourselves are comforted by God.

2 CORINTHIANS 1:3–4 ESV

During difficult times, it can be tough to take your eyes off your own problems and notice the people around you. However, it is just as important to find people who will do the journey with you as it is to become a better person on the journey yourself. When you're going through a difficult stretch, you also have an opportunity to bless and help the people around you. You have the chance to bring your family, friends, and loved ones with you on your journey, to share in what God's doing in your life and show leadership as you authentically and honestly walk the difficult path.

When you're suffering and struggling, you have a spotlight on your life. When Bobbie and I have faced opposition from others, we know that as much as we hurt, our kids always felt our pain a whole lot more, and our church family would also be feeling the weight of scrutiny from neighbors, colleagues, and peers. Knowing we had a chance to exercise faith, especially in the midst of our pain, helped us to focus on God and not on our circumstances. We didn't want our kids to think we had stopped trusting in God's power and goodness just because we hit a rough patch. This was when they needed to see what we believed in action.

Disappointment and hurt is an opportunity to be transparent, but don't be pitiful—and there is a difference. This process can be challenging, compounded by the more people you have watching you. It is at times like these that our human nature is to put on a brave face for those around us, but to vent and even lash out at the people who are closest to us in the midst of heartache. Often spouses are "sacrificed" to our unredeemed emotions during times of anguish and pain—and yet the people closest to us are the ones we need the most. Don't forgo good relationships for a moment of hurt and anger—learn to lean firmly on those who have promised to remain faithful in the good times and bad. This is the example we see in Christ's life, remaining honest and transparent about his pain with those closest to him.

Today's Thought

Sharing the seasons of your life—the enjoyable ones as well as the painful ones—allows God to shine through your responses and bless the lives of those around you.

Today's Prayer

Dear God, you created people in your image to be relational beings. Thank you that we need one another. Today I pray that you will allow me to bless and comfort those in need around me. Help me to remain transparent and engaged with the people in my lives and always to point them back to you. Amen.

Today's Reflection on Living, Loving, Leading

_____

_____

_____

_____

DAY 46
Taking Responsibility

Today's Scripture

Carry each other's burdens, and in this way you will fulfill the law of Christ.

GALATIANS 6:2 NIV

Leadership, at any level, is so often proven in the tough times—there is definitely a strength in revealing yourself as human and vulnerable in these moments without collapsing in despair. By God's grace, he has brought Hillsong through every trial that's ever arisen—continually winding upward rather than spiraling downward—but it hasn't come without a cost. As leaders, Bobbie and I always made the decision to never let the crisis create a bigger crisis. And we never let anything deter us from what God called us to do: love God and love people.

I'm convinced that when you let people know what's going on and where you are at, with transparency and authenticity, they respond positively and want to rally behind you.

This process of transparency does not mean getting defensive and blaming others. When I ride my motorcycle, which is not very often these days, I ride it with the attitude that any potential accident is my fault. Because it's a motorbike, you don't get too many second chances. So in other words, whether someone pulls out in front of me or cuts me off, I'm still the one taking the risk and facing a potential life-threatening accident. So I ride in a posture that makes me responsible for whatever happens to me on the highway. Obviously, I can't control other drivers and their choices and mistakes, but that's part of the risk I assume whenever I choose to ride.

I try to lead the same way, not by blaming others or assuming someone else is at fault but by taking responsibility for my decisions and whatever happens. You can always find reasons why you're not to blame and why you're the victim. But this is no way to lead your life, and it will ultimately undermine the big, spacious life you want to live as you follow Jesus.

Jesus faced unbelievable pressure many times in his ministry on earth—when news of Lazarus' grave illness reached him, when he was tempted in the wilderness by Satan, in Gethsemane, and on the cross—and yet every time he remained focused and unwavering in his Spirit. Satan will use pressure and opposition to try to control you and when we yield to pressure, we surrender our leadership. It is important to deal with circumstances when opposition arises, but don't allow it to control you.

Today's Thought

Taking responsibility for your actions allows you to endure life's trials by focusing on Christ. His life demonstrates the power of real strength required to be a vulnerable leader.

Today's Prayer

Dear Jesus, I want to be a leader who takes responsibility for his actions, a leader like you who remains vulnerable and open to those they serve. Please give me the strength needed to lead and the humility required to serve. Allow me to be a leader who reflects your power and passion in all that I do. Amen.

Today's Reflection on Living, Loving, Leading

_____

_____

_____

_____

DAY 47

Moving On

Today's Scripture

Don't let anyone look down on you because you are young,
but set an example for the believers in speech,
in conduct, in love, in faith and in purity.

1 TIMOTHY 4:12 NIV

Many years ago I came up against one of the most bizarre and unforeseen challenges our church has ever faced. We had just put out a new album, and literally within days we discovered that one of the songs on the album, which was attracting a lot of attention, had been written by someone who was not only living a lie, but had knowingly deceived many people with a fabricated story that evoked people's attention and compassion.

Not wanting to perpetuate this person's deception, we had a difficult decision to make. The immediate impact of these revelations included a huge financial burden and involved recalling thousands of DVDs. The ongoing impact of this deceptive behavior could very well have devastated many lives and the consequences could have been catastrophic both locally within our own church and globally in the Christian community.

However, it was at that time that even though I felt completely duped and disappointed, I had to lead the church in a way that encouraged people who were hurt and confused to rise above the disappointment and find God in the midst of their questions. It wasn't easy, but I called on others to choose to see this person from the perspective of his human frailties and extend forgiveness rather than take offense.

In these moments we can choose to allow disappointment to create a root of bitterness or deep-seated hurt in us, or we can allow it to humble us and extend understanding and love. Such disappointment is an opportunity to evaluate and consider our own lives and the effect we can have on those around us. Even when we don't feel like taking the high road and moving on, we must remember the impact on those around us.

Incredibly, the issue itself was very short-lived within our church. Because I didn't wallow in anger, disappointment, and frustration, others chose not to do so either. In leadership generally, I have learned that if it is a problem to me, it will be a problem to those around me. And therefore it is important to not pretend everything is okay but simply address the issue, shift focus, and move on.

———————————○———————————

Today's Thought

When you move forward by refusing to dwell on unpleasant surprises and the disappointments they cause, you provide true leadership to those around you.

Today's Prayer

Dear Lord, it's not easy to move forward when an unexpected blow knocks me down. Thank you for lifting me back to my feet, dusting me off, and setting me back on your path. I pray I would never wallow in self-pity or blame others. Instead, may I take responsibility to lead with a humble spirit and an open heart—just like Jesus. Amen.

Today's Reflection on Living, Loving, Leading

_____

_____

_____

_____

DAY 48
Lead Courageously

Today's Scripture

Whatever things are true, whatever things are noble, whatever things are just, whatever things are pure, whatever things are lovely, whatever things are of good report, if there is any virtue and if there is anything praiseworthy— meditate on these things.

PHILIPPIANS 4:8 NKJV

One of the best ways to move forward according to God's timing is to focus on his goodness. When we beat ourselves up over what might have happened or what might have been, we miss out on what God wants to give us moving forward and what he wants to teach us in the present.

When we're struggling along in pain, it's tempting to follow the exact opposite of the exhortation we're given in the verse above (Phil. 4:8). When speaking to our congregation I lightheartedly like to make a point clear by highlighting the way our human nature often thinks, with what I like to call my "Opposite World Translation." In this instance it goes something like this: "Whatever things are rumor or hearsay, whatever things are negative, whatever things are mean, whatever things are trashy, whatever things dig up the dirt, whatever things bring a juicy report, if there are any skeletons in the closet, anything gossip worthy, think on these things."

Are you living according to the Opposite World Translation, or are you living according to the Word of God? Because it's good to focus on the positive report when you are surrounded completely by the negative data. Don't say you're focused on God's point of view when you're really looking over your shoulder or at your feet. Look ahead! Look up! And travel on your journey of faith with people who will reset your spiritual compass if it goes astray.

And never forget, ultimately God will bring you through your current trial. He will deliver you from present circumstances and redeem your suffering. And one of the best ways he accomplishes both results is through his people. So when the path grows dim and you feel like giving up, turn to your brothers and sisters, your fellow believers, your local church, and lean on their strength. Let them in to your pain and allow them to share just a little of what you're going through. This is how we get through the hard parts of life. This is how we grow and this is how we lead.

Live transparently.

Love authentically.

And lead courageously.

Today's Thought

Live through crisis with courage and an authority that points people to the One with answers, not the one with problems.

Today's Prayer

Dear God, it can be so difficult to admit my mistakes to others and to let them see me struggle. But every leader must deal with situations that require them to stretch their abilities and to risk failure. In the midst of life's storms, help me to be the kind of leader who provides security and stability for those I serve. Help them to see that it's not through my own efforts but only because I depend on you. Amen.

Today's Reflection on Living, Loving, Leading

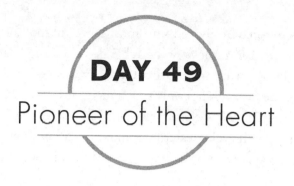

DAY 49
Pioneer of the Heart

Today's Scripture

For the Word of God is living and powerful, and sharper than any two-edged sword, piercing even to the division of soul and spirit, and of joints and marrow, and is a discerner of the thoughts and intents of the heart.

HEBREWS 4:12 NKJV

Imagine losing your brother to an incurable condition. Then imagine discovering the ability to cure the incurable condition. That is exactly what Christian Barnard, a cardiothoracic surgeon from Cape Town, did. He was the first surgeon to ever perform a human-to-human heart transplant in 1967. Years of research from fellow doctors and various experimental surgeries gave him the opportunity to pioneer this lifesaving medical procedure that has undoubtedly changed the face of modern medicine and saved so many lives. Many people would consider him the original heart pioneer, but there was another one even before him.

You see, God himself is not only the original pioneer, creating the heavens and the earth out of the void, but also a pioneer of operating on the human heart. He created the first man and woman, something never attempted or accomplished before he breathed his life into dust to form flesh and blood.

Through the generations that followed, pioneering seems to be in our DNA, which makes sense considering we're made in God's image. John 1:1 says, "In the beginning was the Word, and the Word was with God, and the Word was God." Verse 14 goes on to say, "And the Word became flesh and dwelt among us." There's no mistaking it: From the very beginning, God pioneered!

But he also pioneered by giving us the most powerful tool for operating on the human heart. I love the way the Bible describes the Word of God as being not only powerful, but sharper than a two-edged sword—so sharp that it can divide between not only soul and spirit but between joints and marrow (Heb. 4:12). Now that's precision! The Bible, the Word of God, has the ability—with even greater power and precision than Dr. Christian Barnard—to divide between the thoughts and intents of the heart.

God knows what's in your heart and how to heal you. His Word has the power to operate within your motives, decisions, and responses. Being a pioneer like our Creator, we must be willing to face areas within ourselves in need of healing and then allow him to do just that.

***

Today's Thought

God calls us to be pioneers just like he has pioneered—it's in our spiritual DNA. He has given us his Word to fuel our journey and to heal us when our hearts fail us.

Today's Prayer

Dear God, I am so thankful for your Word and its amazing truth and power. I pray you would continue using it in my life, both to provide instruction on how to live as well as to reveal your character. May it truly be a lamp unto my feet, shining a light so that I can see the next step, and then the next, as I follow you. Amen.

Today's Reflection on Living, Loving, Leading

_____

_____

_____

_____

DAY 50
Pioneered to Prosper

Today's Scripture

Beloved, I pray that you may prosper in all things and be in health, just as your soul prospers.

3 John 1:2 NKJV

The story has been told that after Walt Disney passed away, his wife, Lilly, was at the opening of the newest theme park, Walt Disney World in Orlando, Florida. During the ceremony, one of her friends leaned over and said, "Shame Walt isn't here to see this." To which Lilly replied, "Walt did see this—that's why it's here."

God gives us the ability to dream, to imagine, and to plan so that we might bring those things he has planted in our hearts to life. What do you presently see when you close your eyes? What vision or dream has God planted in your heart for you to nurture and cultivate? What vision sustains you when you're hurting and afraid, shocked and stunned by life's events?

God is indeed a great pioneer, and I believe that he not only gives you visions and dreams, but he always completes what he begins. God doesn't start something in us so that we can live frustrated, restrained, bitter lives. Jesus is called the Author and Finisher of our faith, or as another translation renders it, the Pioneer and the Perfector. God has planted something in you that he intends to bring to fruition if you will just keep your dream and your vision alive. He wants us thriving in the wide-open territory where our souls can flourish! This is particularly important to remember when the path of life becomes difficult.

It's your heart that plans your way and determines your ability to experience the big life God has in store for you. This ability to prosper is not just about material blessings so much as it's about an internal state of peace, joy, and fulfillment in how you live your life. In fact, I believe that when we thrive internally, then blessing can ultimately outwork itself in every area of life.

You see, Jesus pioneers internally and outworks externally. The Bible describes him as the pioneer of our salvation, the pioneer of our faith. And I would describe him as the pioneer of our hearts. Salvation is something that Christ does in our heart that changes our eternal destiny. It changes your reason for being, it changes your sense of purpose, it changes the way you live, it changes the reason for our gifts and talents, it changes our families and our marriages. Ultimately salvation that starts in the heart has an impact on generations to come. But the change starts on the inside, in our heart.

Today's Thought

God works in your heart so you can experience his peace, power, and purpose for your life internally before seeing his impact on the transformation of your life externally.

Today's Prayer

Dear Lord Jesus, today I give you thanks and praise for the way you are transforming me from the inside out. You have given me a big, spacious life filled with dynamic purpose and so many blessings. May I be a good steward of all you've entrusted to me as I seek to further your kingdom and draw others to you. Amen.

Today's Reflection on Living, Loving, Leading

_____

_____

_____

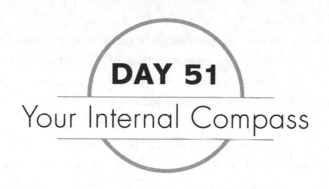

DAY 51
Your Internal Compass

Today's Scripture

My heart is overflowing with a good theme; I recite my composition concerning the King; my tongue is the pen of a ready writer.

PSALM 45:1 NKJV

Every story is written to a good theme—and the theme of your heart determines the story of your life. This can be hard to remember when you find yourself struggling in the midst of overwhelming circumstances and devastating trials. When the path gets difficult, we often have to stop and regroup, to pause and check our directions. Our internal compass attuned to God's spirit is our heart.

But it's not easy to stay connected to God when darkness descends and you can no longer see the path in front of you. It's no wonder we often wake during the night, unable to get back to sleep as we face the worries of the day. David says, "My heart also instructs me in the night seasons" (Ps. 16:7). So many things breed in the night. Fear and anxiety breed in the night. Confusion and discouragement, desperation and discontent breed in the night.

How many times have you awakened from a sound sleep, unable to rest because of all that weighs on you? How many people do you know who have lost their way in the pitch-black of the night season? Yet as we read in the Bible, the theme of David's heart enabled him to say, "The lines have fallen to me in pleasant places; yes, I have a good inheritance. I will bless the LORD who has given me counsel...I have set the LORD always before me" (Ps. 16:6–7, 8).

The way you regain your proper perspective and renew your strength is by returning focus to the great constant in your life—your Savior and his love for you. How you live your life tends to reflect the overflow of your heart. If you lose the vision, the dream that God has planted in you, then you will ultimately lose your way. Especially during those dark nights of the soul, when you can't see your way through life's obstacles, you must return to God's Word and keep your heart fixated on the One who remains the only constant in a world of shifting shadows. He remains the same yesterday, today, and tomorrow and will keep your feet steady when you can't see your next step.

Today's Thought

When trials come and obstacles pop up on life's path,
the way you recalibrate and renew your journey is by
keeping your heart focused on God.

Today's Prayer

*Dear Father, I know that one of the reasons you have given us
your Word is so we can remember your promises and meditate
on your truth. When circumstances close in around me and I feel
surrounded by darkness, I pray I would call on your name
and trust in your Word. Amen.*

Today's Reflection on Living, Loving, Leading

_____

_____

_____

_____

_____

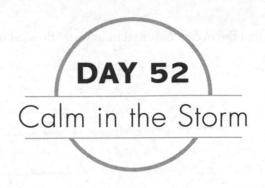

DAY 52

Calm in the Storm

Today's Scripture

The LORD is my rock and my fortress and my deliverer;
my God, my strength, in whom I will trust; my shield
and the horn of my salvation, my stronghold.

PSALM 18:2 NKJV

Bobbie and I had only been married a couple of days when we encountered rough waters—literally! Enjoying our honeymoon on a budget, we had decided to take a ferry from the South Island to the North Island in our native New Zealand. These ferries were enormous carriers, large enough for hundreds of cars in the hull and even more passengers on deck.

Sitting in the front lounge, up three stories high, we faced a spectacular view through huge windows opening onto the bow of the ship. At first it felt as if we were on a roller coaster, riding the waves up and down as they rocked us. Soon, however, the angry dark green waves increased in size and intensity, crashing over the rails of the decks below us. We watched as walls of water formed around us—yes, *walls* of water!

But then suddenly, almost as if in slow motion, a giant wave came from the side. The bow dipped beneath the water, pummeled by the wave's sheer force, and we watched in terror as the wave came up over the decks below us and crashed into the windows of the lounge. Out of natural instinct, we closed our eyes and braced ourselves in our chairs as the wave crashed through the windows and in on us.

After several seconds, Bobbie and I opened our eyes in shock. People began screaming, soaked and bleeding from the broken glass everywhere. The sharp, salty smell of the ocean assaulted us as water flooded into the interior of the ship.

I took Bobbie by the hand and we proceeded through knee-deep water toward the back of the ship. I tried to assure my new bride that everything would be okay, so I said something like "Don't worry, Bobbie, we'll be all right—and if we're not, then we'll be in heaven! It's just a matter of how we get there!" Not exactly the most comforting words, but she knew my heart.

Our captain, familiar with these waters, stopped the boat and let it list until it was safe to make headway again. He knew we had to deal with the aftermath: bail out the water and restore our course settings before we could continue. Thank God we had a captain who was calm in his heart, who not only knew the course and could see the shore, but had prepared for the journey.

How do you handle the rough waters in your life? What's overflowing in your heart right now? Are you willing to declare your trust in God during life's storms? Or are you complaining, grumbling, and despairing when the waves crash in?

Today's Thought

God provides a rock, an anchor, when the waves of life crash in on your life. Rest assured he has already gone ahead and prepared a way through every storm you'll encounter.

Today's Prayer

Dear Lord, when I can't see over the waves crashing around me, I ask that you would hold me close, protect me, and remind me of your constant presence. You are my rock, God, and my security is in you. Thank you that I can rest in the knowledge that you are my refuge and shelter amidst the ups and downs of life. Amen.

Today's Reflection on Living, Loving, Leading

DAY 53

The Dreams of Your Heart

Today's Scripture

"Where there is no vision, the people perish: but he that keepeth the law, happy is he.

PROVERBS 29:18 KJV

Not long ago, I encouraged my congregation to write down the visions of their hearts, the goals they desired to pursue based on God's urging. Their responses ranged from starting new businesses and ministries to moving away to foreign lands and unfamiliar cultures. Some were as simple as talking to neighbors they had never met. Regardless of the size and scope of their heart's dreams, most knew right away what I was talking about. However, despite how quickly they responded, it amazed me how many people told me they were afraid to do it! They had a strong sense of something God had placed on their heart for them to do, and yet they were scared to take the first step.

Can you relate to their dilemma? What is the one thing that God has spoken to you about that you are perhaps too afraid to say out loud? If you could dream a big dream, one that nobody would laugh or scoff at...what would it be? What's keeping you from getting started—right now, today? What are you afraid of?

God plants such beautiful things in our hearts. We often think of secrets in a negative way, and certainly many secrets can be painful, if not harmful. So often we think of secrets as skeletons in the cupboard—things we don't want people to find out. But what about those "secrets" that God has pioneered in your heart, something that's just between the two of you—a desire, a yearning, a longing, something that brings tears to your eyes and stirs something deep down inside you.

There could be so many wonderful things, maybe so many personal things in your heart that God has birthed there. Perhaps the dreams are so tender, so vulnerable, and so personal that you've never told anybody. Maybe you've just told your spouse about some deep longing, some deep belief, some incredible dream that God put in your heart. No matter how impossible it may seem, I can tell you with absolutely certainty that what he's put in your heart he wants to complete in your life. If there's a secret to living the big, wide-open, abundant life, then it all comes back to what's going on inside your heart.

Today's Thought

If you want to experience a long, joyful life, then you must hold tight to the vision God placed inside you—strive less and envision more.

Today's Prayer

Dear Lord, I thank you today for the vision you have given me and the goals you have set before me. At times they seem too big, and I'm not sure how I can keep going or how they will ever be accomplished. But I only have to focus on the step you ask me to take today. You continue to strengthen me and to provide all I need to fulfill my calling. Thank you for the ways you stretch me to realize my full potential. Amen.

Today's Reflection on Living, Loving, Leading

_____

_____

_____

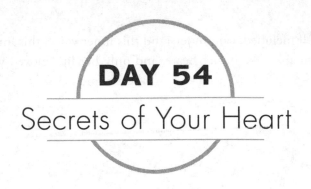

Today's Scripture

Be strong and take heart, all you who hope in the LORD.

PSALM 31:24 NIV

Long before there were a few dozen people meeting in a schoolroom in a suburb of Sydney, long before there was a Hillsong Church in Australia, let alone one in more than a dozen other countries, I saw this vision in my heart: an outpost of grace, a church so large the city could not ignore it—a healthy, functional, and glorious Body of Christ.

Now we've seen God do so many amazing things, it exceeds anything I could've imagined. Nonetheless, I've held on to that church that we pioneered inside my heart ever since I was a young man. Were there times when I thought we might never make it? Of course! But I never lost sight of the vision in my heart.

Someone else who never lost sight of her heart's vision is Hannah. She had a burning desire to have a child, even though it seemed physically impossible. Married to a man named Elkanah, Hannah struggled with anger in her soul and a sharp, jagged pain in her heart over her situation. But she refused to give up her hope, the vision of birthing a baby boy that God had planted in her heart. Scripture describes her persistent petition this way: "And it happened, as she continued praying before the LORD, that Eli watched her mouth. Now Hannah *spoke in her heart;* only her lips moved, but her voice was not heard" (1 Samuel 1:13, emphasis added).

Isn't that a fascinating way to phrase Hannah's petition before God? "Now Hannah spoke in her heart." I wonder exactly how that works, although all of us, myself included, can understand this inner voice, this inner burning desire. Hannah spoke in her heart, and only her lips moved without any sound coming from her mouth. Eli, the temple priest, assumed she was either a crazy woman or drunk!

When have you felt like Hannah in your desperate desire to hold to the vision God has given you? Sometimes when you can't verbalize all that God has placed in your heart, you struggle to give voice to it. You can't articulate it, and worry that if you try it would only sound silly or stupid. Maybe those who heard it wouldn't understand and instead would think you were bragging or even delusional. But what God places in our hearts is so precious and beautiful, we must hold those secrets closely and guard them.

Today's Thought

If what the Lord has deposited in your heart has not produced
fruit, don't give up. Just keep the hope alive in your
heart and guard it.

Today's Prayer

*Dear Heavenly Father, you have placed dreams and desires within me
that are unique to my passions and purpose. Fan the flames of those
dreams, Lord, that I may fervently pursue their completion through
your power and in your timing. Give me patience when I'm forced to
wait along with all I need when it's time to move forward. I praise
you for the special and secret dreams of my heart. Amen.*

Today's Reflection on Living, Loving, Leading

DAY 55

A Sigh of Surrender

Today's Scripture

Trust in him at all times, you people; pour out your hearts
to him, for God is our refuge.

PSALM 62:8 NIV

Years ago, my mum told me a story of a time I would have been too young to remember. My father, who had been a Salvation Army officer, was unemployed, and not only that, he was unemployable—due to two recent nervous breakdowns. My mum was raising five children in one room, was penniless, and had a husband who had lost all perspective and vision and had no means of support. Her perspective was bleak to say the least and her faith was being stretched to its limits.

One day, she told me, when she was hanging out the clothes in the backyard at our home there in New Zealand, she literally flung herself in despair over the clothesline and cried out to God, "I can't take this anymore!" Well, God met her in that place. She recalls slumping over with a sigh—desperate for answers from the Lord. She had reached her limits and cried out to God to meet her right there in that moment, which he did. It was a while before circumstances improved, but my mother had a sense of God's presence and peace that assured her all would be well.

What does her cry of desperation represent to you? And her sigh of surrender? What is it in your life that you currently don't understand, feel in despair about, or can't come to terms with? Because the very same pioneer who authored your salvation can also renew faith in your heart—and the power of faith in your heart can lead to a breakthrough in your life. You may feel like giving up and your current obstacle may seem impossible to overcome, but all things are possible for God.

What's your longing? That tender, vulnerable thing that you can't even give words to? What have you been afraid to cry out to God about? No matter what you're going through or have endured, he is faithful to hold you close. No matter how lonely, angry, desperate, or disappointed you may feel because of circumstances or the actions of others, you can count on your Heavenly Father to hear the cries of your heart.

Today's Thought

Pour out your heart to him, for God is your refuge.

Today's Prayer

Dear Jesus, sometimes I reach my limits and I don't know how I'll keep going, let alone lead others who are in my care. On those occasions, may I always cry out to you and trust that you will hear me and meet me in those desperate moments. I don't have to know all the answers or be able to see the road ahead. I only have to rely on you. Thank you, Lord, for showing me the way. Amen.

Today's Reflection on Living, Loving, Leading

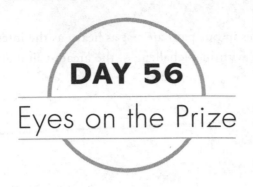

DAY 56
Eyes on the Prize

Today's Scripture

I press toward the goal for the prize of the upward call of God in Christ Jesus.

PHILIPPIANS 3:14 NKJV

Sometimes we have no choice but to hang on and let life's "waves"—unpredictable circumstances like sickness and death, financial hardship, and unexpected loss—crash over us. In those moments we often feel caught off guard and blindsided by such unexpected disaster. But then we have to be like the captain of the ferry Bobbie and I were on. We have to assess the damage, remediate and resolve as much as we can, and then refocus our attention and energies on where we're headed.

We have to make sure our heart's setting is on what God wants for us, what he has instilled in us, and what he wants to develop in our lives. We have to let go of the fears, doubts, and regrets that so often plague us in the midst of a crisis. Once we've reestablished where God is leading, we must move forward without delay.

As you consider taking the next step and then the next when the path gets difficult, you often discover that you must pause and reset your course. When life gets hard and the waves are crashing around you, you can't stick your head in the sand and pretend otherwise. But you also can't allow the storms of life to capsize your journey permanently. It can be tempting to just stop and make excuses and then keep stalling instead of starting up again.

This temptation to get stuck in fear and self-pity reinforces why we must pause only long enough to restore our proper vision. Many times, the external obstacles in our path are not as heavy as the internal ones. When we're struggling with life's challenges, the greatest limitation we face may come from the issues of our heart.

If we're not guarding and protecting what God has placed within our hearts, then we lose our vision and find it difficult to persevere. Over time we become skeptical and uncertain, even doubting the accuracy of what we know God has revealed to us. The vision you have for your life must be protected in your heart. When you encounter a difficult path, you must keep your eyes on the prize.

Today's Thought

When terrible events sidetrack you from your journey,
you must take time to refocus your destination, renew your
energies, and return to the path God has for you.

Today's Prayer

*Dear Lord, you know how challenging it can be when obstacles
block my path. Sometimes I get discouraged and don't know what
to do or how to keep going. In these times, please remind me to
trust in you and to keep my eyes on the prize. Today I just have to
take the next step and then the next. Thank you for guiding
me and illuminating my path. Amen.*

Today's Reflection on Living, Loving, Leading

DAY 57
Keeping Hope Alive

Today's Scripture

I have learned in whatever state I am, to be content: I know how to be abased, and I know how to abound. Everywhere and in all things I have learned both to be full and to be hungry, both to abound and to suffer need. I can do all things through Christ who strengthens me.

PHILIPPIANS 4:11 13 NKJV

December 27, 2012—I remember the day well, because Bobbie and I were flying out that day from Sydney to the United States, and before we went to the airport, we met with Joel and Esther (my eldest son and his new wife) for breakfast. There they shared the joyful news that they were pregnant. We were overjoyed!

After our excited chatter and all the questions and congratulations, we went to pay for our breakfast, only to find that someone had already taken care of the bill! I assumed another diner must have overheard our great news and wanted to treat us in celebration, but I had no idea who it was.

Fast-forward one year later to that very day—December 27, 2013—I was going for a jog around the coastline when a young stopped me and said, "Excuse me, Pastor Brian, can I tell you a quick story?" So I quit jogging and this young man walked alongside me and began to tell me this story:

"Twelve months ago my wife and I were in a little café in Bondi having breakfast. We were desperate. We were desperate because we couldn't have children and we were hoping and believing that against all odds we were going to have a baby in the New Year. It was there in that café that we

179

decided we were going to fast for the first thirty days of the New Year, and we had just made that decision when both you and Bobbie, Joel and Esther walked in and sat at the table almost right next to us."

He went on to tell me that he overheard Joel and Esther share with us their great news, and he admitted that in all honesty, it kind of hurt. There they were as a couple talking about their desperation and the longing of their hearts, only to overhear and witness someone else's joy. He said that despite the hurt they felt, they paid our bill anyway.

He continued, "We did what we said we were going to do, and we fasted for thirty days. And well, God heard our prayer...and here she is!" As he was telling me this, a beautiful little two-month-old baby looked up at us from where she was strapped to a carrier on his chest. My eyes got moist as he shared with me their determination to hold on to the dreams in their heart and God's faithfulness in their desperation. God pioneered something in their hearts—and what he pioneered in their hearts, he completed in their lives.

Today's Thought

When we give thanks for what God has done in our lives—
and what he's about to do—we resist envy and defeat despair.
Thanksgiving keeps our hearts focused on God's
goodness for our lives.

Today's Prayer

Dear Jesus, I confess that sometimes when I see others with something I want but don't have, it's tough. Envy sets in and jealousy, along with frustration, anger, and resentment. If I'm not careful, I become bitter and give the enemy a greater foothold to distract me from all you have for me. Calm my heart, Lord, and remind me that I have all that I need through you and your power. Help me to rejoice with those who are celebrating your blessings. Amen.

Today's Reflection on Living, Loving, Leading

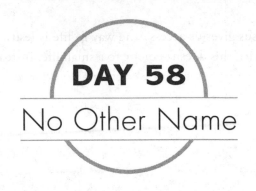

DAY 58
No Other Name

Today's Scripture

"Salvation is found in no one else, for there is no other name under heaven given to mankind by which we must be saved."

ACTS 4:12 NIV

After the song "No Other Name" was written by my son Joel and Jonas Myrin, we (as a church) began to camp around the name of Jesus and the all-encompassing power, majesty, beauty, and holiness held within his single name, and its effect on our lives today. In fact, our creative team created a kind of lyrical poem, an epic statement asking everyone to consider the significance of names and the utter uniqueness, power, and holiness contained in the name of Jesus. One of my favorite passages proclaims:

NO OTHER NAME changed nature, mind-sets and matter.

Opened blind eyes, deaf ears and healed cancer.

NO OTHER NAME came with this mandate:

Heaven's Kingdom expressed on Earth.

"No Other Name" lyrics *Iseme Adeola, aka Isi the Scribe*

We were captivated by considering the way no other name in history contains so much power, freedom, and hope. Shortly after "No Other Name" was penned, we decided to focus our live worship album and Hillsong Conference around these very thoughts and images.

The name of Jesus gives us access. The way to life is Jesus. Only Jesus. But for those in Christ, this doesn't equate to a small life. Instead, in Christ, life becomes larger, wider, more full of potential and blessing than any other way will ever allow us.

I think that far too often people mistakenly correlate the difficult path with being a restricting and constricting path—but the Bible doesn't say that! They falsely assume because life gets hard that their lives must be more limited and confined, which is not the case at all. We read throughout the Old Testament that David's journey was at times intensely difficult, but in 2 Samuel 22:37, he says, "You enlarged my path under me; so my feet did not slip."

The path may be difficult, and the gate may be narrow—but let me tell you, there is a whole lot of life to be accessed through that narrow gate! His name is JESUS. And as we step into grace and through the narrow gate, he leads us into a life of glorious potential.

Today's Thought

The name of Jesus not only has the power to save you from your sins and set you free, but it also has the ability to expand your life in the most joyful, satisfying ways.

Today's Prayer

Dear Christ Jesus, today I marvel at the power of your name and the way you dispel darkness through your glorious presence. Thank you for reminding me that some people make the gate seem narrower than it actually is. Help me to follow and trust you as my passage through this gate into eternal life. Amen.

Today's Reflection on Living, Loving, Leading

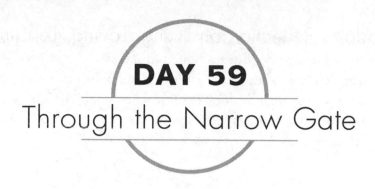

DAY 59
Through the Narrow Gate

Today's Scripture

*"I am the way, the truth, and the life. No one comes
to the Father except through Me."*

JOHN 14:6 NKJV

One name remains foundational to our ability to live the big, abundant life God wants us to have: Jesus. We may not stop to think about the implications, the meaning, the power behind Jesus' name, but it's essential if we want to reach our divinely appointed destination. In fact, Jesus didn't leave us much choice as evidenced by his statement in the verse above.

And notice Jesus didn't say that he's the tour director or the traffic cop for the way to know God. He said that he is the way. While I have no doubt that our path to knowing God is found only through Jesus, I also know that the message of the gospel is inclusive, not exclusive. Jesus invites everyone—men and women, Jew and Gentile, rich and poor, young and old, everyone—to accept the gift of grace by confessing that one and only name. While Jesus declares that he is the only way (exclusive), he opens his way up to all who call upon his name (inclusive). He's as inclusive as he is exclusive—it's the subversive nature of the gospel, the upside-down way of the kingdom, and good news for everyone.

So in order to enjoy the spacious, wide-open life Jesus came to bring and that we can access and enjoy in him, we have to believe him when he also said, "Enter by the narrow gate; for wide is the gate and broad is the way that leads to destruction, and there are many who go in by it. Because narrow is the gate and difficult is the way which leads to life, and there are few who find it" (Matt. 7:13–14).

Jesus makes it clear here that it's not going to be easy or convenient or popular to follow him. So the gate to life and abundance is narrow—Christ makes that clear here—but I fear that sometimes we make the gate tighter and more confining than he does. Because when we follow him, we don't have to worry about squeezing through or scraping along. Jesus has gone before us and opened the way for us.

Today's Thought

The key to unlocking the narrow gate is Jesus. There's no other name. He alone is the way.

Today's Prayer

Dear Lord Jesus, I thank you today for the power of your name and the new life I have through you and your death on the cross and resurrection. You are the way, the truth, and the life, and I praise you for saving me and setting me free. Help me to trust that you have unlocked the narrow gate so that I can pass through it into the eternal presence of God. Amen.

Today's Reflection on Living, Loving, Leading

DAY 60
Name Dropping

Today's Scripture

"And I will do whatever you ask in my name, so that the Father may be glorified in the Son."

JOHN 14:13 NIV

We can't deny that names carry great power by what we associate with them. Most of us have a funny relationship with our names. We may not even think about them very often, but they usually serve as our point of reference for the people around us. We name people to distinguish them, to identify them, and perhaps to honor something larger (a family, a business, a heritage) of which they are part.

My name is Brian Charles Houston. It has served me well as far as names go. My identity is in my name, not spiritually speaking, but as I live out my life on earth as a man. My credibility is in that name. My reputation is in that name. My authority is in that name. To give someone else authority, my authority, I sign my name.

Recognition is carried in my name. It does have some limitations, however. My name won't get me automatic access to Buckingham Palace or the White House.

But my name does get me in to certain places.

For instance, I was recently flying out of Sydney and my daughter her little boy, Jack, my grandson, were with me. At the time Jack was still nursing, so my daughter looked for a private spot, and so I suggested that she come with me to the airline's club lounge.

188

Greeting the hostess there, I introduced myself and explained the circumstances. "Well, Mr. Houston," she said apologetically, "we're really not permitted to do that...and I shouldn't even consider it, but for you, of course we can."

So my daughter was allowed to enter the exclusive lounge area and wait along with me in a quieter, more private setting. She couldn't do it on the power of her own name, but in this case my name got her in. Obviously, she wouldn't have tried to gain entry on her own because she knew the club rules.

Unfortunately, we sometimes forget who made us and empowers us and can do anything. Instead we try to rely on our own efforts and run up against the limitations of our own name. However, we can enter into the fullness of life, even though the gate is narrow, because we have the authority of the name of Jesus. Just as Laura gained access because she's my daughter, we belong to a family with much more clout, influence, and authority: the family of God.

Today's Thought

There is not one thing in your life—no challenge, no problem, no heartache—over which you cannot speak the name of Jesus and see victory.

Today's Prayer

Dear Lord, I'm grateful for my name, its meaning, and the practical purpose it serves. But I'm most grateful for the power of your name and the access I have into God's presence because of it. Today I will reflect on the name of Jesus and the power it brings into all areas where it is spoken. Amen.

Today's Reflection on Living, Loving, Leading

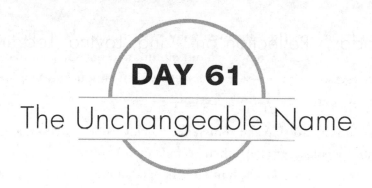

DAY 61

The Unchangeable Name

Today's Scripture

*Therefore God also has highly exalted Him and given Him
the name which is above every name, that at the name of
Jesus every knee should bow, of those in heaven, and of those
on earth, and of those under the earth, and that every
tongue should confess that Jesus Christ is Lord,
to the glory of God the Father.*

PHILIPPIANS 2:9–11 NKJV

Since we have started new churches around the world—in cities like London, Kiev, Dusseldorf, Paris, Cape Town, New York, and most recently in Los Angeles—we might be tempted to assume that the Hillsong name is drawing people. But this would be a huge mistake. The name Hillsong may initially attract people, but it will never save anybody!

Don't get me wrong; we're blessed to have a recognized name that God has graced, like Hillsong. It's our name and God has blessed us with this name. In fact, I know Hillsong is perhaps a bit of a weird name for a church. You might have guessed by now that it didn't emerge from the original Hebrew or Greek text, and you won't find Hillsong in the Bible. No, we pioneered our little church in an area of rolling hills in Sydney's Northwest called the "Hills District." It's about as simple as that.

When we began to produce our very first live worship albums I realized that people might not buy music titled "Hills Christian Life Centre Worship" (reflecting our original church name)—it just didn't roll off the tongue. So I got together with our team, and we sat and brainstormed what these projects could be called—and eventually everyone settled on "Hillsong." At the time, this brand encompassed our albums and our small annual music and creative conference—so each advertisement we put out would invite people along to these "Hillsong" events.

But as both the worship and conference quickly gained traction, and more and more people came along, there seemed to be confusion about the name of the church. So we got the hint and changed our name. And the rest—as they say—is history.

Needless to say, we are proud to be part of this global church community, and we thank God that he's given us influence through the Hillsong name.

But the real influence, the real power source of every ministry ever attempted by Hillsong, has nothing to do with the name that is over the door of our church. The real influence and power source comes from the One who is our focus and Savior. Any impact we have comes from the Son of God, Jesus. He is who we worship, who we follow, who we look to guide us. His name is above every name and has power above every other name. It's never been about a church called Hillsong—it's always been about a Savior called JESUS!

―――――――○―――――――

Today's Thought

Names are important—for people, for churches, businesses, and institutions. But the only name above all others, the only name with the power to forgive sins and save lives, is Jesus.

Today's Prayer

Dear God, too often I overlook the amazing power I have through the name of Jesus. Like a compass on my journey of faith, it restores me and heals me, guides me and comforts me. Today I ask that I may bring the name of Jesus to those people around me who need salvation and who long for purpose in their lives. Amen.

Today's Reflection on Living, Loving, Leading

DAY 62
Your Savior's Name

Today's Scripture

That power is the same as the mighty strength he exerted
when he raised Christ from the dead and seated him at
his right hand in the heavenly realms, far above all rule
and authority, power and dominion, and every name
that is invoked, not only in the present age
but also in the one to come.

EPHESIANS 1:19–21 NIV

The power of Jesus' name is continually echoed throughout Scripture. The Bible also makes it clear that even demons have to recognize the power of the name of Jesus. His name causes all knees to bow and all tongues to confess the truth of who he is.

In the Jewish culture, the name Jesus literally means "Jehovah is salvation," which we often translate as "savior." The name came from God himself when he sent the angel to visit Mary with the amazing news that she would be the mother of God's Son. The angel told her, "Do not be afraid, Mary, for you have found favor with God. And behold, you will conceive in your womb and bring forth a Son, and shall call His name Jesus. He will be great, and will be called the Son of the Highest; and the Lord God will give Him the throne of His father David. And He will reign over the house of Jacob forever, and of His kingdom there will be no end" (Luke 1:30–33).

My name has limitations and so does yours. If we only live according to our own authority and influence, then we're always going to run up against our limitations. That's why the only hope we have comes from the name of

Jesus. His name is the narrow gate, and we have the right to live and operate under that great name above all names. This is the best news possible, especially regarding those problems for which we don't know the answers. We often face obstacles in life and feel squeezed off the faithful path of following Christ. We get so close to what the future holds, and yet we don't have any access to it. We can't find the trail that leads to this place God is calling us to reach, and we're not sure which next steps to take. That's where the power of Jesus' holy name becomes our key.

His name is strong, and yet tender. Fierce and yet gentle. It's trustworthy and sincere, powerful and merciful, and the declaration of its limitless ability could go on for eternity. The best news

of all is that you and I have inherited it as joint heirs, brothers and sisters of Jesus. We have a legacy of power, purpose, and possibilities we've barely tapped into. The gate may be narrow, but Jesus always makes a way for those living under his oath of salvation, his promise—those traveling by his unchanging, unshakable name.

Today's Thought

Do you want to know the way to get through the narrow gate?
The name of Jesus—there is no other way, there is no other name!
So much meaning, power, history, and authority
contained in that one name!

Today's Prayer

Dear Jesus, no other name but yours contains such power and authority over heaven and earth. I'm humbled when I consider that you are my Savior and I have access to you on a first-name basis. Thank you for being a personal, relational, caring God. Thank you for allowing me the privilege of carrying your name into all the world so that everyone may know the joy, peace, and power that comes from Jesus Christ. Amen.

195

Today's Reflection on Living, Loving, Leading

DAY 63
A Desperate Plea

Today's Scripture

The centurion replied, "Lord, I do not deserve to have
you come under my roof. But just say the word,
and my servant will be healed."

MATTHEW 8:8 NIV

After almost two years of growing consistently from week to week, our church had outgrown the little school hall where it all started for us, and we began to look for a new, larger meeting space. It was a stretch, but we leased a brand-new warehouse in the same area.

During our transition into this new space, our offices were located on a mezzanine floor upstairs above our open meeting room, and while there was a railing around the stairwell, its posts were more decorative than substantial. There really wasn't much to keep someone from falling over or even sliding in between the rail posts.

So I was sitting in my office one afternoon when I heard a sickening thud. Immediately, I thought, "Oh, please, Lord, I pray that wasn't Ben." My son was about two at the time, and he would often visit the offices while Bobbie and I worked. Sure enough, when I ran out to the stairs, I saw Ben lying on the ground floor below, a cold concrete floor with no carpet or padding of any kind.

Dashing down to my son, my little boy, I realized he wasn't breathing. I felt sick, absolutely terrified. Each moment seemed frozen, as if I couldn't do anything for him fast enough. Ben's pale skin was growing even whiter, tinged with a bluish-purplish color. A small stream of blood trickled from the back of his tiny head, where I knew it had to be fractured.

I wasn't sure I should move him, but I also couldn't stand seeing him lying there on that cold concrete floor. So instinctively, I scooped him up in my arms and held him close to my chest as I screamed the only name I could utter, "JESUS!"

It was a prayer, a plea, and an urgent summons for help, the cry of a beggar pleading to keep the most precious gift he has—of a father who would take his son's place in an instant. Miraculously and immediately Ben flickered his eyes and began to breathe again. I don't know whether it was the shock he got from such a loud scream, but I like to believe that it was truly the power that's in the only name I could call on in that instant.

It turned out that Ben did indeed cut his head and fracture his skull. In fact, he still has the scar to this day, but praise God there was no permanent damage done that day. I have no doubt that the only word I could utter, the name of Jesus Christ, saved him.

Today's Thought

When you're desperate and feel powerless, the name of Jesus is the only name that matters.

Today's Prayer

Dear God, when I find myself powerless in the face of danger, disaster, distress, or disappointment, I will call on the name of your Son, Jesus. When I reach my limits, when I need a miracle, when I can see no other way, I pray the name of Jesus will rise from lips. He alone has the power to provide all I need— both today and forever. Amen.

Today's Reflection on Living, Loving, Leading

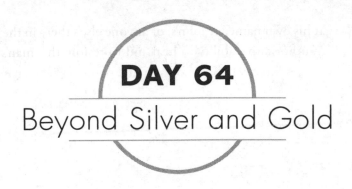

DAY 64

Beyond Silver and Gold

Today's Scripture

"Silver and gold I do not have, but what I do have
I give you: In the name of Jesus Christ of Nazareth,
rise up and walk."

ACTS 3:6 NKJV

While we find numerous examples and demonstrations of the power of Jesus' name in the Bible, one of my favorite scenes occurs in Acts. In the third chapter we find a couple of Jesus' disciples on their way to the temple in Jerusalem to pray. Entering through a portal called the Beautiful Gate, so named according to first-century historian Josephus because its beauty shone beyond gold and silver, Peter and John encountered a lame beggar.

For forty years, every day of his life, this crippled man was taken to the Beautiful Gate. He could sit there and beg next to it, but he wasn't allowed to enter into the temple courtyard like the many Jewish people who had a certain status. For all its magnificent beauty, this gate might as well have been a stone barricade or an iron curtain.

The lame beggar saw Peter and John about to enter the temple through the Beautiful Gate, and he called out to them for money, doing what he did there day in and day out. The two disciples noticed the man, asked for his complete attention, and then told him that they didn't have any money. "Silver and gold I do not have," Peter said. But then he gave the beggar something priceless, commanding him to rise and walk in the name of Jesus Christ of Nazareth.

Notice that Peter wasn't trying to live according to what he did not have.

200

He knew that his own name, or John's, or anyone else's there in the city, did not have the authoritative ability to heal and to restore this man's lifelong ailment. But Peter knew what he did have: the power of Jesus' name.

Too often we can get fixated on what we lack and forget what we actually do have. Through the name of Jesus, we have all we will ever need. Even though he had no money, Peter knew the precious worth of his Master's name. He knew the name of Jesus, like the Beautiful Gate of the temple, was beyond gold and silver.

Today's Thought

We don't have to be lame or physically impaired, like the man at
the Beautiful Gate, to experience healing in the name of Jesus.
The value of his name transcends all the gold, silver,
and precious jewels the world has ever seen.

Today's Prayer

*Dear Lord, so often I'm tempted to place value on material
possessions and judge other people's worth by what they own
or the amount of money they make. Forgive me for losing
sight of what is of eternal value. Remind me that I
already have the most valuable gift anyone can have:
the name of Jesus over my life. Amen.*

Today's Reflection on Living, Loving, Leading

DAY 65

It's Who You Know

Today's Scripture

Then Peter, filled with the Holy Spirit, said to them: "Rulers and elders of the people! If we are being called to account today for an act of kindness shown to a man who was lame and are being asked how he was healed, then know this, you and all the people of Israel: It is by the name of Jesus Christ of Nazareth, whom you crucified but whom God raised from the dead, that this man stands before you healed."

ACTS 4:8–10 NIV

As a product of our human nature, we tend to love to name-drop—you know, mention the celebrities we've met, spotted at the airport, caught a glimpse of at our favorite restaurant, or sat next to at a charity dinner. Maybe in an effort to seem more glamorous and important or to pretend our lives are more exciting by association, we enjoy mentioning who we know or have met.

However, as we see in the encounter Peter and John had with the lame man at the Beautiful Gate (in Acts 3), there's only one name truly worth dropping: Jesus Christ. Only the name of Jesus has the power to heal lives and to change hearts. Peter and John could not do it on their own any more than you or I could've healed that lame man. They knew what it meant, though, to pass through the narrow gate of a seemingly impossible situation. They knew what it meant to trust God for the impossible.

So as Peter helped lift this once-lame man up off the ground to stand on his own feet, the man discovered a state of physical health—pain-free legs—that he'd never known. With such healing power coursing through his body, this newly restored man had no choice but to praise God. Finally able to go through the Beautiful Gate, he could finally enter this place of prayer, praise, and worship in the presence of God.

But the lame man's story of healing didn't end there. Leaping and shouting with joy, this man went with Peter and John into the temple courtyard to a section known as Solomon's Porch (in Acts 3:10–11). When everyone marveled to see the lame beggar up and walking, Peter knew that he couldn't take credit for this miracle and wouldn't have dreamed of trying.

But giving credit to Jesus, who at this point had already been arrested, crucified, and resurrected, didn't go down so well with the Jewish religious leaders who wanted Christ killed in the first place. So it was no surprise that the guards known as the Sanhedrin, there at the temple gate, immediately arrested Peter and questioned him. They wanted to know what everyone there wanted to know: "How did you make this guy walk again? By what name? In whose power? In whose authority? What's really going on here?"

Peter made it undeniably clear that the only name capable of such a miracle is the name of Jesus. He proclaimed the power of the name of Jesus and wanted everyone there and then as well as here and now to recognize its limitless authority.

Today's Thought

We don't have to rely on knowing celebrities, meeting wealthy leaders, or rubbing elbows with movie stars to know our value. Through the name of Jesus, we can claim our identity as sons and daughters of our Heavenly Father, the King of creation.

Today's Prayer

Dear Heavenly Father, I give you thanks and praise today for the ways you are transforming me into the image of your Son. My identity rests solely in Christ Jesus. Thank you that I don't have to impress anyone or feel insecure around other people. Because I have the name of Jesus, you have made me a joint heir with him of all your heavenly blessings. Amen.

Today's Reflection on Living, Loving, Leading

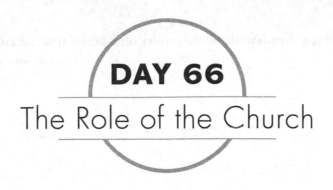

DAY 66

The Role of the Church

Today's Scripture

So then you are no longer strangers and aliens, but you are fellow citizens with the saints and members of the household of God, built on the foundation of the apostles and prophets, Christ Jesus himself being the cornerstone, in whom the whole structure, being joined together, grows into a holy temple in the Lord. In him you also are being built together into a dwelling place for God by the Spirit.

EPHESIANS 2:19–22 ESV

The disciples' healing of the lame man at the Beautiful Gate offers us a lovely, concise picture of the role of the Church: to lift people up, using our own strengths and abilities, so that the power of God through the name of Jesus Christ can heal them, restore them, and enable them to know God's love. This is the model upon which we based Hillsong.

As a young pastor starting out, I realized that if my preaching and teaching was always aimed at building and lifting the lives of those I was speaking to—rather than being polarized around exhorting people to help me fulfill *my* vision and build *our* church—then Jesus would build *his* church. It has always been my goal to build not only people's spiritual lives but also their everyday lives—to preach to their Mondays, not just their Sundays. This includes lifting the lives of the broken and needy, reaching out to both the poor in spirit and the poor.

For years, our church has endeavored to see the need, both within our own walls and externally, in our local community and beyond. The need is great, but it has been the unhindered generosity of believers that has enabled the work of the kingdom and the name of Jesus to go forward into places we never could have envisioned or imagined.

Today, children in Mumbai are learning to read and write, are being fed and clothed and educated—and they are giving the next generation of their society hope for the future. Entire communities in Africa have been impacted through the generosity of the Church, and we've seen schools and houses, feeding programs and jobs, rise from the mud plains and poverty, bringing joy to families. Men and women have been saved, rescued, and prevented from entering the sex-trafficking industry as we've partnered with others to educate and prosecute people involved, and end this horrific crime against humanity.

The Church of Jesus Christ around the globe must be committed to seeing lives changed, families strengthened, cities transformed, and future generations positioned to make a difference. It is through this work that we have the opportunity to not only lift people's lives but to introduce them to the saving reality of Jesus Christ. All we do as Christians, as the church, is only through the power of his holy name.

———————◯———————

Today's Thought

As the Body of Christ, his church, we are Jesus' hands and feet
on earth, feeding, serving, healing, and saving through the
power and authority of his name.

Today's Prayer

*Dear Father in heaven, thank you for allowing me to be your hands
and feet here on earth, loving and serving those in need. Today help
me to see those individuals you want me to serve in your name.
I pray I will glorify you in all that I do. Amen.*

Today's Reflection on Living, Loving, Leading

DAY 67
Unlimited

Today's Scripture

Praise be to the God and Father of our Lord Jesus Christ!
In his great mercy he has given us new birth into a living
hope through the resurrection of Jesus Christ from the dead.

1 Peter 1:3 NIV

Through the name of Jesus, we have the same access to God's power that his disciples in the Bible had. Tragically, many times we live in the limitations of our name rather than in the freedom we have through the name above all names. We settle for less and assume we've reached our limits, that the best days of our lives are already behind us. We struggle to believe that the best is truly yet to come.

And if we live only according to the name we're given or the name we choose for ourselves, then we face insurmountable limitations. Even if we're a famous celebrity, a notorious public figure, or royalty, we still have the limitations of our humanity. Simply put, it doesn't matter who we are or what our name may be—we're still limited.

Only one name elevates us beyond the limitations into which we're born. It's the name that can cause us to go where we've never gone; to do what we've never done or even imagined ourselves capable of doing. It's a name equally personal as it is powerful, as intimate as it is universal, both exclusive in being the only way to God and yet totally inclusive in its invitation to all people, both Jew and Gentile, male and female, slave and master.

The name of Jesus can unleash power in your life unlike anything you've ever experienced. It can open doors, close wounds, and reveal a path across the waters of a wind-tossed sea. His name allows us to burst beyond the limitations of our own names and our own abilities.

The hope we have in the name of Jesus is an anchor for our souls, a bridge both sure and steadfast uniting heaven and earth. Our relationship with Jesus takes us straight out of this natural world and directly into the eternal realm of the presence of God. If we genuinely believe that his name is higher, that his word is greater, and that his power makes all things possible, then our anchor will keep us secure no matter how much the storms of life rage around us.

Today's Thought

When you face disappointment and discouragement, when you wonder if your best is yet to come, call on the name of Jesus and trust in his promise to be with you always. When you trust in the Name above all names, your future is truly unlimited.

Today's Prayer

Dear Jesus, my trust rests in you and you alone. Forgive me for those times when I momentarily lose my way and pursue sinful idols and dangerous addictions. Thank you for restoring my soul and granting me mercy. May I always cherish the name of Jesus. Amen.

Today's Reflection on Living, Loving, Leading

_____

_____

_____

_____

_____

DAY 68
An Anchor for Your Soul

Today's Scripture

This hope is a strong and trustworthy anchor for our souls.
It leads us through the curtain into God's inner sanctuary.

HEBREWS 6:19 NLT

A few years ago, two of our young songwriters from Hillsong here in Sydney, Ben Fielding and Dean Ussher, began working on a song inspired by the verse above (Heb. 6:19). Like many songwriters do, they set it aside after getting stuck on lyrics and melodies and began working on other tunes.

Only a few weeks later, however, Dean and his wife Rachel suffered a miscarriage, and this unfinished song became so much more personal. Both Ben and Dean knew that they had to finish what they started. Despite the circumstance, this Scripture had become a great reassurance in the midst of such loss and pain. Both songwriters committed to crafting the lyric around Hebrews 6 and came up with a song they called "Anchor." In God-orchestrated coincidence, I was scheduled to preach that week on the promise of God, his promise to Abraham and now to us.

Hebrews 6 treats our present hope and the unshakable nature of God's promise as inseparable. It speaks of two unshakable things: God's promise and his oath (his name). The hope that anchors the soul is the hope in the fact that God not only desires to fulfill his promise but is completely able to. He kept his word through the death and resurrection of Jesus. He has given us his name as a seal on his promise. His name is greater and higher than even the most overwhelming circumstance. When all is shaken, his word and the power of his name remains unshakable.

It is through the name of Jesus that you can find a new beginning and a new day, a new hope and a reassurance of a glorious future. God loves you and he is on your side. He sent his only Son to save you from your sins. Yes, the gate is narrow but it is also beautiful. Through the power of Jesus' name, your foot is already in the door.

Even when you fall and gasp for breath, one name holds the power of life. One name lifts you up again and again. One name is the anchor to our soul. One name holds the answers to sickness and death, holds the keys to blessing and future hope.

Only one name: Jesus.

Today's Thought

Whatever your next step may be, whatever circumstances you might face, may the name you call upon be the One who will always answer: Jesus.

Today's Prayer

Dear Lord Jesus, today I pray that your name will always rise up within me whenever I'm tempted to slow down, give up, or despair on my journey of faith. You are my anchor and my hope, my bridge to the Father, and my key through the narrow gate. Grant me your power to bring your hope to everyone I encounter. Amen.

Today's Reflection on Living, Loving, Leading

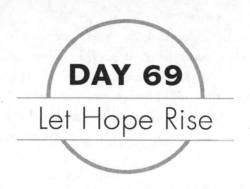

DAY 69
Let Hope Rise

Today's Scripture

*Beloved, now we are children of God; and it has not yet been
revealed what we shall be, but we know that when He is revealed,
we shall be like Him, for we shall see Him as He is.*

1 JOHN 3:2 NKJV

"Why would anyone want to see a movie about us?"

This was my response when some Hollywood producers approached Bobbie and me with a proposal for a Hillsong movie. We were intrigued to say the least, and over lunch with them while in Los Angeles, where we had recently planted a new church, they shared their vision for a film project. It would be a "rock-umentary" style movie highlighting some of the all-time favorite songs from Hillsong's thirty-year journey, with behind-the-scenes insight into the songs, stories, and the songwriters, all through the lens of Hillsong UNITED. They clearly had put a great deal of thought into their pitch and seemed genuinely enthusiastic.

Bobbie and I shared their vision with the rest of our Hillsong team, and after some discussion, we began to move forward with the making of the movie *Hillsong: Let Hope Rise*. It was surreal to find ourselves in the offices of Hollywood distributors and financiers over the next few months, and interviewing potential movie directors—each of whom had built impressive résumés after directing some highly successful films. By God's grace, we saw all the pieces miraculously come together.

Sharing our journey from a school hall in the Sydney suburbs to a church graced with growing congregations in many of the world's great cities, the film gives viewers the opportunity to experience the impact of the praise and worship that God has birthed through Hillsong Church. We knew it would be hard work, particularly for the UNITED team and their families, not to mention the sometimes awkward situation of having cameras pointed at us constantly. Yet, when all was said and done, we could not pass on the opportunity to point others to the One we live for and long to glorify: Jesus.

We could never have imagined making a movie about ourselves and Hillsong's journey over the last few decades, but God sure did—and he made it happen. We've already heard many amazing personal stories about how he's using *Hillsong: Let Hope Rise* to draw viewers to knowing him, including some of the filmmakers. Reluctant at first, we realized once again God was leading us into new, unfamiliar territory, stretching our faith and blazing new trails.

Today's Thought

The longer you follow in the footsteps of Jesus and allow God to lead you, the more open you will become to the surprising ways he will use you to further his kingdom and deepen your faith in the process.

Today's Prayer

Dear God, you always know how to surprise me by using people, events, and circumstances to reveal yourself. May I always remain open to new ways of spreading the name of your Son, Jesus. May I always be willing to risk my temporary comfort for an eternal legacy. Amen.

Today's Reflection on Living, Loving, Leading

_____

_____

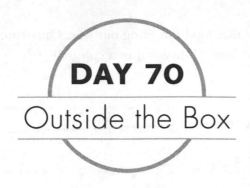

DAY 70

Outside the Box

Today's Scripture

"God, who made the world and everything in it, since He is Lord of heaven and earth, does not dwell in temples made with hands. Nor is He worshiped with men's hands, as though He needed anything, since He gives to all life, breath, and all things."

ACTS 17:24–25 NKJV

Sometimes I have to shake my head in amazement at the days we are living in and the way the world has changed. Over the years I've witnessed many Christians spending their time and energy worrying about external practices and religious matters that really didn't have a lot to do with loving God and loving people! The judgmental attitudes of a small minority, who force their perhaps well-meaning but ill-informed opinions on others ends up preventing many from ever entering a church building or calling upon Jesus' name.

For example, I grew up in an era when we were told by our church pastors, elders, and even parents that you shouldn't go to the movies in case "Jesus came again and you were in the movie theater." Apparently, Jesus didn't go to the movies! This example of small thinking does nothing for the gospel message, and even today we see these kinds of attitudes giving Christians a bad name.

If we live our lives in such a narrow way, believing what so much of the world continues to believe about Christianity—that it is meant to be kept small and quiet, represented by dilapidated buildings filled with narrow-minded, self-righteous finger pointers—then we will never find ourselves with all the opportunities that God can bring our way. Opportunities like a local church partnering with Hollywood in a culturally relevant way to spread the good news!

In the same way, films, multimedia, lights, and loud music aren't for everyone, and my firm belief is that relevance is not about the clothes you wear, the type of music you sing at your church, or the kind of car you drive. True relevance is measured by the distance between what you say and what you do. If your actions and lifestyle fail to line up with what you say, preach, and believe—then your message becomes irrelevant. However, if we live our lives in a wide-open way and remain relevant in terms of the definition above, we will see opportunities with spiritual eyes and attract the favor of God.

This means we cannot narrow our view of what serving Jesus looks like! What I've come to learn over many years is that the favor of God is sometimes unexplainable and outside of the box of the "safe" and "comfortable" Christianity some people seem to prefer. I don't for one minute believe that we need to conform to the world in order to make ourselves attractive to the unchurched. The message of the gospel is sacred, but I believe the methods have to change.

───────────── ○ ─────────────

Today's Thought

God wants us focused on sharing the good news of the gospel of Christ in ways that appeal to others, like a sweet aroma, not alienating them by criticizing them for cultural practices.

Today's Prayer

Dear Father God, forgive me when I criticize popular culture or post less than positive comments online or on social media. Remind me that I am a child of the King, saved by the power of Jesus' name. Empower me to be a beacon of hope and grace to a world brimming with darkness. Thank you for being my light and my salvation. Amen.

Today's Reflection on Living, Loving, Leading

DAY 71
Open and Expansive

Today's Scripture

We didn't fence you in. The smallness you feel comes from within you. Your lives aren't small, but you're living them in a small way. I'm speaking as plainly as I can and with great affection. Open up your lives. Live openly and expansively!

2 CORINTHIANS 6:11–13 MSG

I have often said I'd rather be a musician than a music critic, a moviemaker than a movie critic, a chef than a food critic; and I'd rather be a church builder than a church critic. I would prefer to live my life as the kind of person who engages with the world of film and television, who spends money on the sound system so that Friday nights at youth group compete with any good party down the road, and who puts in the extra effort to graciously swing wide the doors of our church for activities during the week so that people who may never dream of coming to a Sunday service feel welcomed, loved, and cared for.

Open and expansive—or, in other terms, compassionate and embracing, gracious and all-encompassing. With social media so pervasive now, I continue to be amazed at the number of angry people who identify themselves as Christians but who have nothing positive, hopeful, affirming, gracious, or compassionate to say about anyone or anything. There are some particularly harsh and judgmental critics who seem determined to pick on people through Instagram, Twitter, Facebook, and comment forums, criticizing every form of faith and ready to publicly deride others with differing viewpoints.

My friend Phil Cooke calls people like this "armchair theologians"—those who hide behind their computer screens and look for "issues" to point out to fellow believers, all under the guise of biblical accountability. They see themselves as a kind of theological compass, ready to point out anything that seems amiss, off course, or simply not in line with their own understanding of the Bible. This isn't living openly and expansively at all, and more important, it bears no resemblance to the grace-filled way Jesus lived his life on earth. Ironically, Jesus saved his harshest words for the religious.

As a leader, I value the need for accountability and constructive feedback from colleagues and peers, from friends with relational and ministerial credibility who would take the time to reach out in care and correction. These conversations can make us better as leaders if we maintain a teachable spirit. However, it is probably wise to pay very little attention to the anonymous and mean-spirited attacks of those who may never have subjected themselves to accountability and correction. We must follow God's leading and not the whims of public opinion.

Today's Thought

The example of Jesus is inclusive, compassionate, inviting,
hopeful, and positive. We must resist temptations to play
"armchair theologian" and commit to being on the
front lines of living the wide-open adventure of
faith to which we're called.

Today's Prayer

*Dear Lord, it's so tempting to play it safe and allow others to
take risks while I observe, spectate, or criticize from the sidelines.
Forgive me for those times when I've stayed too comfortable
rather than following you to the front lines. Give me the power
today to step out boldly so that others may know
the name of Jesus Christ. Amen.*

Today's Reflection on Living, Loving, Leading

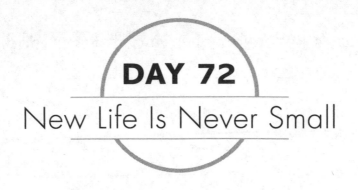

DAY 72
New Life Is Never Small

Today's Scripture

Therefore, if anyone is in Christ, the new creation has come:
The old has gone, the new is here!

2 Corinthians 5:17 niv

Only a few short years ago, I believe God spoke to me about the timing of planting our very first Hillsong Church in the United States. There has always been something about big cities with lots of people that has beckoned my attention. By God's grace, Hillsong Church is flourishing in all of the big, world-class cities where we are planted.

I knew, long before we ever began there, that New York would be one of those cities, and I've since learned that Carl Lentz and my son Joel (as twenty-one-year-olds in Bible college in Australia) had dreamed of one day starting a church together in NYC—a city that had previously been labeled a "graveyard" for churches. You see, despite the many great churches and pastors serving God already in this amazing "city that never sleeps"—where new nightclubs and restaurants are opening by the dozen—there are also many churches that are going "out of business." Many people warned us of this reality, and of the perils of planting in such an ungodly, transient, large city—and yet we knew that God had always opened doors for us if we were in tune with his Spirit, listening for his leading, and were in the right place, at the right time, with the right people.

Five years on, Hillsong New York City is thriving. We are consistently filling over seven services each weekend and seeing people line up around the block to hear the truth of the gospel. One of my favorite parts of Hillsong

New York is seeing the diversity of the crowd each Sunday. From the faceless to the famous, the Word of God and passionate worship is touching people's lives in that city and changing them from the inside out. We are serving alongside other great churches and ministries in New York, and together we are seeing this concrete jungle and "church graveyard" come to life in the power of Jesus' name.

Paul told the Corinthians that "smallness" comes from within us, and not from God. The "smallness" we felt in such a big city could have hindered what God wanted to do if we had allowed it to navigate our thinking. But we knew God had in mind something much bigger than we could even imagine.

Today's Thought

Many people will tell you why you cannot succeed in your endeavors, but God will fulfill your dreams to overflowing if you remain faithful to his calling for your life.

Today's Prayer

Dear Jesus, today help me focus on the many blessing you bestow on my life, especially in those unexpected places and surprising relationships. Too often, I accept the mindset of others and limit what I think I can do. But you remind me that all things are possible—things beyond my wildest dreams— through the power of your name. Amen.

Today's Reflection on Living, Loving, Leading

_____

_____

_____

_____

DAY 73
Spacious Living

Today's Scripture

So spacious is he, so roomy, that everything of God finds its proper place in him without crowding.

COLOSSIANS 1:19 MSG

The gateway to knowing God feels tight and constricting only when we try to do it on our own. When our human mind can't comprehend the miraculous work of Christ, then instead of allowing his grace and saving power to awe us, we criticize that which we don't know and shrink back from that which seems unknown. Rules, limits, regulations, and discipline become a burden only when we're forced to obey and understand in our own power, which we simply cannot do.

But through Jesus we have freedom and life, purpose and power, joy and peace. The narrow gate will never make you a smaller person—because you will never come second by putting God first.

When amazing things happen in our lives, some people may try to explain them away or find a "rational" reason. If they can't make sense of us because they have reduced the narrow gate to the size of a keyhole to match their own biases and limitations, then we must be gracious, loving, and respectful in response. We have to realize that in our everyday lives, through our churches, through the situations in which God places us, people will usually be confounded by a testimony that doesn't make sense to them. When we're part of something that's not the result of our own power, others can only scratch their heads.

And even when you're actively and accurately reflecting who Jesus is, even when you're revealing the wide-open, spacious life he brings as we pass through the narrow gate, some people will be drawn to God through you. They will realize something different about you, something that's not about who you are or what you're doing, but something supernatural, a glimpse of Christ. They are hungry to know God, so when we have the opportunity to heal, to preach, to teach in Jesus' name, we must not back down.

Others may try to silence you—either because they claim to know God but don't represent him truthfully, or because they don't know him and simply cannot understand the things of God. But because of the power we have through Jesus Christ, we will always be compelled to speak the truth of who he is and what he's done for us. So if someone approaches you one day about making your life into a movie that reflects what Christ has done—don't rule it out!

Today's Thought

Where God's Spirit opens doors, we must keep walking,
knowing that the gate is narrow but not constricting.

Today's Prayer

*Dear God, you delight in exceeding people's expectations and
bursting through their defenses. Thank you for the big, spacious
life you have given me through Jesus. I know that this new life I
have in Christ has no place for small minds or narrow thinking.
I praise you for my larger-than-life faith. Amen.*

Today's Reflection on Living, Loving, Leading

_____

_____

_____

_____

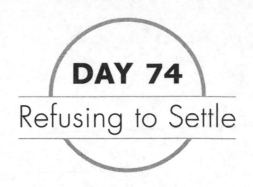

DAY 74
Refusing to Settle

Today's Scripture

The LORD gives strength to his people; the LORD
blesses his people with peace.

PSALM 29:11 NIV

On my worst days, when I feel overwhelmed and stressed, I often imagine how nice it would be to step back and get a job with no pressure. I remember once watching somebody mowing a field on a tractor, with that beautiful aroma of freshly cut grass that accompanies spring, and I thought, "Imagine a job like that! When your biggest stress is whether or not you have enough gas to finish mowing the field." Those thoughts never last long, though, because I have an overwhelming sense that I am to live called, not just saved.

In those moments when I'm tempted to settle for less than my calling, I remember an old pastor who pioneered a church in Sydney in the early 1920s or '30s, and he continued to minister, preaching and pastoring, well into his eighties. As the story goes, he had just finished preaching one Sunday morning, and the congregation closed the service with the hymn "Within the Veil I Now Would Come." And that was just what he did! The old preacher passed from this earth to heaven right there in the same church he pioneered! Could there be any better way to go?

I admire his determination to his calling to share the gospel, and while I don't want to be doing all I do today in my eighties, I do pray that as long as I have breath I will live with a sense of calling and purpose. I want to find joy and passion in mentoring others, and setting up generations to build upon the foundations we (and those who have gone before us) labored to build.

Isn't this how you want to live your life? Filled with passion and excitement, with the confident knowledge that you're making a difference in the lives of others, contributing your efforts to God's kingdom for his eternal purposes?

It's rarely easy, but I have always found it satisfying when I'm following the example set by Jesus, led by God's Spirit, fulfilling the purpose for which he made me. As we've discovered, this process is an ever-unfolding adventure, filled with unexpected challenges and miraculous surprises, both the trials and joys drawing us deeper in love with Jesus.

———————◯———————

Today's Thought

Are you content to live saved? Or is your commitment to
live called? I believe "calling" takes away the option of
simply "settling down."

Today's Prayer

*Dear Lord, I confess that sometimes I'm tempted to settle for less
than all you have for me. I get tired and stressed and begin to feel
so exhausted. But you've promised to sustain me and to lighten my
burdens along the path of faith. Help me to let go of all the weight
I carry needlessly. Help me to trust you with my load. Amen.*

Today's Reflection on Living, Loving, Leading

_____

_____

_____

_____

_____

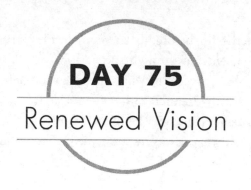

DAY 75
Renewed Vision

Today's Scripture

Surely the righteous will never be shaken; they will be remembered forever. They will have no fear of bad news; their hearts are steadfast, trusting in the LORD.

PSALM 112:6–7 NIV

In the early years of our ministry, when our children were young, Bobbie and I could hardly afford a vacation, let alone take time away from our small but growing congregation for one. Yet early on we learned the importance of time away with our children, and we began to make wonderful holiday memories even with our limited resources.

I remember many summer days taking my boys out deep into the ocean waves and encouraging them to climb onto my back and hold on for dear life as we bodysurfed together to the shore. For a few days, the stress and pressure of being young pastors in a new country and planting a new church seemed to melt away in the heat of the sun. Such times of refreshment allowed us to return to our ministries with a renewed sense of purpose and vision.

We should never underestimate the significance of what we think about ourselves, the calling and purpose we hold on to that drives our lives forward. We must avoid burning out by taking time to rest and be refreshed. Otherwise, we risk losing our vision for the adventure of faith to which God calls us. When we don't have confidence in God's plan and purpose for our lives—when we walk through life without vision—we are walking a dangerous line.

Paul led a destructive life before his encounter with Christ on the Damascus road, before he entered through the narrow gate. Although he stayed his edgy self after his conversion, Paul's lifestyle was realigned so he would become a builder of the Church rather than a destroyer of it. Everything that was in him beforehand was bent on destroying the Church, but in Christ he found out what it was he was called to do; in Christ he found a personal vision.

Perhaps, like Paul, you think you've gone too far down the wrong road, made too many bad decisions to ever live a life of wisdom and discretion. Maybe you feel as if you've completely lost your way and can't find the way out, or maybe you've just made a few poor choices along the difficult road. Don't despair! It's *never* too late to make changes and choose again God's path for your life. His way is Jesus (see John 14:6) and his Word is the light that shows you the direction to go (see Ps. 119:105). God's grace will relocate you onto the right path and establish your life on a foundation that will stand in a time of storms and teach you how to make wise decisions for a glorious future.

Today's Thought

Life is full of choices, and the choices you make will determine the course your life takes. But God's way— the narrow gate—will always point you in the direction of his purpose and fulfillment.

Today's Prayer

Dear Lord, today I give you thanks and praise for the many ways you sustain me and the ministry to which you've called me. Sometimes I feel badly for not doing more or for wasting opportunities in the past. But with you, I know my best is yet to come, and that you will continue to keep me steadfast in my faith. Amen.

Today's Reflection on Living, Loving, Leading

DAY 76
Resisting Temptation

Today's Scripture

No temptation has overtaken you except what is common to mankind. And God is faithful; he will not let you be tempted beyond what you can bear. But when you are tempted, he will also provide a way out so that you can endure it.

1 CORINTHIANS 10:13 NIV

Often our hardest decisions are the small ones, the incremental ones, the choices that seem harmless enough in the moment. The big temptations we often identify and resist, but the really big issues of life usually begin with small choices. No one wakes up one day and thinks, "Today I'll settle for less," or "Today I'll take a break from following God and just wait and see what happens." No, instead the enemy tends to chip away at us in small moments of weakness. A shortcut here, a compromise there, a quick detour now and then—this is why we must remain focused on the example Jesus set for us.

Even though he came to earth on a mission as the Son of God, Jesus faced the same temptations that we face, including the temptation to settle. Our enemy tempted Jesus with the same opportunities to settle for less than God's best that the devil tempts us with today. The scale is different, but the essence of the temptation is basically the same.

In Matthew 4, the devil challenges Jesus to question his very identity. Twice he says, "If you are the Son of God…" Can't you just hear the taunt there? "If you're really who you claim to be, then you should be able to turn stones to bread and jump off cliffs!" But Jesus knows how to wield the Sword of

Truth, and he resists the devil's attempt to test him. He responds with just the right counterpoint from Scripture to reveal the devil's shortsighted, warped logic. "Away with you, Satan! For it is written, 'You shall worship the Lord your God, and Him only you shall serve'" (v. 10).

Jesus resisted the devil's temptations by relying on the truth of God's Word—our greatest resource. Whenever we begin feeling as if we're not talented enough or smart enough, that we don't have enough support or resources, that we should lower our expectations and settle, then we must return to what God's Word tells us. The Bible assures us that we can do all things through Christ, that we are more than conquerors. God tells us that he will supply all our needs according to his limitless resources. We have to remember what's true and not what feels true in the moment.

Today's Thought

Don't listen to the enemy. When you keep your eyes on Jesus, then the gate is more than wide enough for you to pass through.

Today's Prayer

Dear Jesus, sometimes I feel discouraged because I still give in to the same old temptations. I know you forgive me and that I can quickly get back on my feet. When I remember that you have faced the temptations of the enemy in the desert and overcome them, I know I have the power and strength to resist those things that seem to ensnare me. Today, Lord, I pray for your strength to overcome any and all temptations that come my way. Amen.

Today's Reflection on Living, Loving, Leading

DAY 77

The Legacy of a Big Life

Today's Scripture

We will not hide them from their children, but tell to the coming generation the glorious deeds of the LORD, and his might, and the wonders that he has done.

PSALM 78:4 ESV

In order to resist the temptation to settle, let's lead our lives so the fruits of our labor live long after our physical bodies have perished. In order to build God's eternal kingdom and leave this kind of legacy, we have to remain pioneers fueled by grace, committed to explore the wild territory to which God calls us, whether that's the kindergarten classroom, the mission field in another country, or the boardroom at our workplace.

Every field has its pioneers who dedicate their lives and careers to innovation and experimentation. It might be in a laboratory or on a laptop, in outer space or an inner office. It's the commitment to be the best you can be at what you're called to do. It's identifying your passions and pursuing them with a lifelong curiosity. It's leading when it would be easier to follow someone else and following God when you want to go your own way.

Pioneers take risks and take the first steps toward a new discovery, often an unknown one. They invent what they need as they go along, using the resources God provides and not dwelling on what they don't have. They step into something new, and they believe that God will keep his promises and provide the resources to realize the possibilities for greatness in their lives.

Innovating, not settling for less, means allowing God to expand your imagination, increase your wisdom, and multiply your resources so that your energies can be sustained and extended. Not for your own glory, but for God's. When you serve God by leading a big life, it not only blesses you but provides opportunities for others to be blessed as well.

The mission of God at its finest is when we are quenching the deep thirst and ongoing need within the human soul. We lead a big life not for our own fame and fulfillment but so that we can lead others home, home to the house of God, the Church, here on earth and home to the eternal home awaiting us in heaven. When we embrace our big life, living from our God-given purpose with passion each day, we discover the rich satisfaction of being who our Creator made us to be, doing that which he made us to do.

Today's Thought

As long as you follow God's calling on your life and remain true to the pioneering wonder of his Holy Spirit, your life will overflow with joy, meaning, and God's very best.

Today's Prayer

Dear God, I may not always feel like a pioneer in my faith, but I know you continue to stretch me so that I will depend on you more completely. Today I pray you would renew the calling you have placed on my life and refresh my spirit with your presence. Amen.

Today's Reflection on Living, Loving, Leading

_____

_____

_____

_____

_____

DAY 78
Calling over Comfort

Today's Scripture

It was for this He called you through our gospel, that you may gain the glory of our Lord Jesus Christ.

2 Thessalonians 2:14 nasb

Hillsong has been nicknamed "the church that never sleeps." In many ways, it's a true depiction of a house that is always open, always moving from one event, one service, one location, to the next. We are always looking for the next thing, the new thing that God wants to do. When we stop to celebrate, it is a temporary pause, because we are not content to rest on the triumphs of the past but are always looking to the future.

Our continuous growth over the years has inevitably brought with it growing pains. I will never forget the first Friday night gathering in Paris—the city of lights, the city of love, where historic cathedrals are visited daily by tourists, but rarely by worshippers. More than 40 percent of the French population claim they have no spiritual belief at all, but this didn't deter us from what we felt God was calling us to do.

On the evening of our first Paris service, Gary Clarke, our London lead pastor, and I caught a cab to the venue that was less than a block from the Pompidou Centre and only a short distance from the Louvre and the river Seine. As we got one or two blocks from the square, a lineup of people appeared in the distance, standing in the cold and winding around the block. I turned to our host and asked what these people were lining up for. I was astonished to discover that they were trying to squeeze into the small theater we had rented. It was impossible to get everyone in, and to this day I don't know where all those people came from!

Lines have now become a feature of so many of our congregations as buildings struggle to contain the growth. Whether outside the Dominion Theatre in London's West End, or outside the Hammerstein and the Manhattan Ballroom in midtown Manhattan, or even outside the Belasco Theater bringing new life to downtown Los Angeles. These are problems we never imagined we would have, and that those who have gone before us prayed for…good problems, growing pains.

In many ways, these growing pains don't give us room to settle because they require miraculous answers and provision, day to day. The stretch on new leaders, the urgency to create volunteer teams and disciple new Christians are the kind of struggles that can become overwhelming and, at times, uncomfortable. Yet when things get uncomfortable we can choose to focus on the end goal: salvation, discipleship, and God's glorious future.

Today's Thought

No matter how difficult the path gets, how distant
the vision, or how uncomfortable the stretch—
always choose calling over comfort.

Today's Prayer

*Dear Lord, I admit there have been times when my comfort
has temporarily come before my calling. Forgive me for those
times when I've settled for less than your best for my life.
Today help me to see with my eyes turned toward
eternity, not toward myself. Amen.*

Today's Reflection on Living, Loving, Leading

DAY 79
Firmly Planted

Today's Scripture

The righteous shall flourish like the palm tree: he shall grow like a cedar in Lebanon. Those that be planted in the house of the LORD shall flourish in the courts of our God.

PSALM 92:12–13 KJV

If you want to cultivate the kind of big life modeled by Christ, if you want to flourish in your personal vision and calling, and enter into a glorious future, then it requires putting down deep roots. This is a biblical truth we find throughout Scripture. Your calling and vocation are at risk of being swayed, uprooted, or led astray during those inevitably uncomfortable moments if you are not grounded in truth and watered by accountable relationships and encouraging teaching.

For me, when it comes to flourishing in your calling, church is a nonnegotiable. I recognize that church looks different for everyone, but planting yourself in a community of believers who can build up, challenge, and encourage you in your calling is imperative. And I'm not talking about just being a "show-up-on-Sunday Christian."

Just like the healthy tree, if we are to flourish and produce fruit, we have to have our roots down deep in order to receive regular nourishment. Being present and building meaningful relationships with other believers has a significant impact on both our relationship with God and our future.

For many people, finding their place in the family of God is where they will also discover their calling, or gain a sense of purpose in their vocation. But don't be discouraged if this takes time, or you are not yet feeling planted or fruitful. It's hard to stand in front of any tree and actually see it growing before our eyes. Life, faith, and serving Jesus is like that; we can't always see what God is doing in the present moment, but we have to trust that if we are being faithful to steward our calling, he is providing all we need to continue growing.

Just like a tree, a flourishing life is a fruitful life; it will show signs of growth and health: foliage, fruit, flowers, and seeds in abundance. The tree itself will become strong and resilient, rising above the storms of life to also provide shelter for others. When we live according to the purposes of God, when we don't simply live saved, when we plant ourselves in the good "soil and water" of godly relationships, sound teaching, and the truth of God's Word, we will see the fruit of our lives produce more than we could ever imagine.

Today's Thought

When we root our lives in service to God's calling, within
the community of the church, we will flourish and
produce good fruit.

Today's Prayer

*Dear Heavenly Father, today I count my blessings and thank you
for the ways you nourish my soul. I pray that my fruit may
be pleasing to you and that it furthers your kingdom by
reflecting your grace and love to all people. Amen.*

Today's Reflection on Living, Loving, Leading

_____

_____

_____

_____

DAY 80
A Promise Fulfilled

Today's Scripture

"I will make you exceedingly fruitful; and I will make nations of you, and kings shall come from you. And I will establish My covenant between Me and you and your descendants after you in their generations, for an everlasting covenant, to be God to you and your descendants after you."

GENESIS 17:6–7 NKJV

I grew up with pastors for parents, and our home was often filled with guest evangelists and preachers who were ministering in New Zealand and required hosting. On one particular occasion, a friend of my mum and dad, an evangelist from Fiji, was staying at our home and decided to do an impromptu Bible study with my little sister and me. I remember he opened the Bible to Matthew 1 and began reading out loud the forty-two generations of family names, from Abraham to Jesus, found there.

As a child, I could barely understand the lesson he gave that day, but I have never forgotten his enthusiasm. It was so obvious to me that he could see and understand something that I could not. Years on, I can understand the significance of what all those biblical names represented: a promise fulfilled.

We don't have to wait long when reading through the Bible to find God's generational promise to his people, his generational promise to *you*. God uses generations, works through generations, and is undeniably committed to the generations. The faithfulness of our God is not confined to a generation, but it passes from one to the next.

The very purpose of God choosing Abraham and his descendants was so that God might be made known, evidenced through their lives and witness. God has proven himself since his first promise to Abraham, and we have seen it outworked in the generations that followed. Centuries later, the death of Jesus Christ on the cross and his resurrection delivered us this message of generations.

As believers, when we choose to walk through the narrow gate, we stand as heirs to this very same promise made to Abraham. God promised Abraham that his goodness and blessing would be recognizable, and that same promise extends to our generation and the generations to follow. God still chooses to build into generations—and I believe it is through the power of community, the intimacy of relationship, and the vehicle of the Church that he is continuing to reveal who he is to the world.

His continued promises are both personal and universal, directed to individual lives forming his Church, the Body of Christ. God's promises extend beyond the personal ones we have in our hearts and unite us all in the hope we have in Jesus.

Today's Thought

In the Body of Christ, we are all connected in a great network of spiritual relationships, and God uses us—one generation after the next—to help each other along the path of faith and through the narrow gate.

Today's Prayer

Dear God, the saints who have gone before me provide so much inspiration on my own spiritual journey. I praise you for the ways you empowered and sustained them, and I ask that I would be willing to take the same risks and step out in faith just as boldly as they did. Today give me courage to make decisions with a greater awareness of their eternal impact. Amen.

Today's Reflection on Living, Loving, Leading

DAY 81
The Power of Partnering

Today's Scripture

One gives freely, yet grows all the richer; another withholds what he should give, and only suffers want. Whoever brings blessing will be enriched, and one who waters will himself be watered.

PROVERBS 11:24–25 ESV

Individual success is an illusion; anyone who claims sole credit for the successes of life allows pride to deceive them. Behind even the most seemingly individual triumphs there are coaches, teachers, lecturers, family, friends, mentors, an opportunity created by another. Dependability leads us into community and not away from it. It is in community (relationship and partnership) that we discover the needs of others, and we respond by being dependable and trustworthy stewards of what we have been given, good stewards of our holy calling; the result is then thanksgiving and community with God. When we are in relationship with our Heavenly Father, God gives us his Spirit to empower and equip us to do what he would do.

The fact is, our God is all-sovereign, all-powerful, and able to do absolutely anything, and yet he chooses to use us, to lean on us. And I believe that when we lean on and in to others, open our hands and open our lives, God smiles. Because he sees that we have learned something of who he is and what he intended.

I am a great believer in the power of partnership. At Hillsong Church there is an incredible emphasis on being a people known for turning generously toward need and never away from it, for choosing each other over individuality.

Years ago, an amazing family came into our church. Barry and Lynn Denton had four boys, and they began attending Hillsong out of a desire to surround their children with a strong peer group and an active youth ministry.

Many years on, when these boys had become young men and begun businesses of their own, two of the brothers made a decision to stretch themselves and begin a development company; their professional skills complemented each other, and their vision for the future was cohesive. Their love for God and commitment to build his House led them to align their calling to a greater cause—and they attached their vision to ours.

After a few years, the two brothers' skills and hard work, accompanied with their determination and faith, resulted in their business partnership giving one million dollars to the work of the church in a single year. This is the power of partnering with generosity in mind.

I believe your success and effectiveness in life, love, and leadership hinges on your ability to partner with the strategically placed people alongside you for the adventure—people who are willing and able to carry the vision, run the race, and serve Jesus together.

Today's Thought

Following Jesus, you become part of relationships and
partnerships marked by God for future calling
and undeniable purpose.

Today's Prayer

*Dear Lord Jesus Christ, you made it clear that you love a
cheerful giver, someone who is willing to offer all they have
to you and to those in need. You set the example by giving the
ultimate—your life. Today I pray that I may be able to give
generously to those in need. Thank you for all the resources
you've entrusted to me; may I used them according to your
purposes to advance your kingdom. Amen.*

Today's Reflection on Living, Loving, Leading

DAY 82
Future Forward

Today's Scripture

Blessed are those who fear the LORD, who find great delight
in his commands. Their children will be mighty in the land;
the generation of the upright will be blessed.

PSALM 112:1–2 NIV

A number of years ago, just a few short months apart, I visited the former churches of two very prominent world-renowned pastors who had graduated to heaven. Both of these churches now had their sons at the helm, entrusted with the leadership and momentum of their flourishing ministries. One of the sons I had the opportunity to visit with (and subsequently form a relationship with) has honored his father every step of the way, while quietly getting about being true to himself and changing so much of what his father had established. He has risked doing ministry different than his dad, and the result has been staggering growth and influence for their church.

The other son, however, tried desperately to keep his father's name and ministry alive and worked to prop up the past, rather than build for the future. As I spent time there, it was startling to see everywhere the sad reminders of past days of blessing—and to look around and realize that present momentum had come to a grinding halt and things were clearly lacking life and forward motion. It was like a museum exhibit honoring a past achievement, not a living, dynamic, vibrant ministry.

The difference? One honored the past but built for the future. The other lacked vision for the future and tried to rekindle the past.

The truth is that the message of Jesus Christ is timeless, and it is as relevant today as it was some two thousand years ago. However, the challenge for all of us is this: How do we ensure that this generation hears the message in a relevant way—in the midst of the thousands of other voices vying for their attention?

Our ability to blaze a trail for others relies on those who have gone before us. Ultimately, we can trace it back to those first followers of Jesus in the early church. They had no idea they were launching a movement that would change the course of history for centuries to come; they were simply being obedient and following as God's Spirit directed them.

Today's Thought

You're called to honor the past, especially the foundations laid by past generations of believers, but you're also called to create something new with the resources you've been given.

Today's Prayer

Dear God, sometimes I struggle to let go of the past and the way I've grown accustomed to ministering. But I want to remain open to new ideas and new ways of sharing the gospel to reach men, women, and children in today's world. Today grant me the wisdom and discernment to know when to let go, when to hold on, and when to take a leap of faith in a new direction. Amen.

Today's Reflection on Living, Loving, Leading

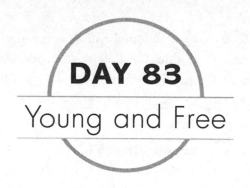

DAY 83

Young and Free

Today's Scripture

Instead of Your fathers shall be Your sons, whom You shall make princes in all the earth.

<small>PSALM 45:16 NKJV</small>

I remember talking to my daughter, Laura, a number of years ago, about Hillsong UNITED. They were once a youth band, but their lives have since grown; now many of them have children of their own, yet they're still fulfilling their dreams, breaking records, and innovating new sounds and lyrics for worshippers throughout all the continents in the world. Deep in my spirit, despite the continued success of Hillsong UNITED, I felt that it was time to pioneer again with a fresh Jesus generation—something that would connect with the hearts of young people still of school age.

It started late one evening in the summer, after an appointment at our City Campus on a Friday night, when I walked into rehearsals for Wildlife—our youth group for high schoolers. I was amazed by the young seventeen-year-old standing on the stage leading worship as if there were thousands in the room, though in reality the auditorium was absolutely empty. I went home inspired to tell Laura who, along with her husband, Peter, are our youth pastors.

As I described my experience, she told me that Aodhan, the young man I had seen, was not only a worship leader but also a songwriter. That night I had seen him rehearsing one of his own songs. In a sense, it was at that moment, and in that conversation with Laura, that Young and Free was born.

Young and Free is a vibrant band, once again built from the talent within our own youth. It has fresh sounds and willing and wide-eyed Jesus-loving young people, who are sparking a whole new movement among teenagers and young adults. Their worship has brought fresh life into our own church and an incredible sense of excitement as people watch the generations grow stronger.

I have always said that I want our church to be the kind of church that is committed to empowering the generations and releasing them to do even greater things than my generation, or those that have gone before. As the verse above (Ps. 45:16) proclaims, *"Instead of your fathers shall be your sons."*

I believe as a church we are called to be making princes in all the earth— kingmakers. We are to be bringing people, both men and women, young and old, inside the body of Christ into their God-given destiny; helping them to live a wide-open, spacious life and build toward a glorious future.

Today's Thought

We are to take the message of Jesus and see his kingdom move forward, stronger, into each generation.

Today's Prayer

Dear Jesus, after you ascended into heaven, you promised to send your Holy Spirit so that we might know you dwell in us, empower us, and comfort us at all times. In your Word, the Spirit is described as a mighty wind, a breath of fresh air filling our souls. Empowered by your Spirit, I pray you will use me to be a breath of fresh air to my neighbors, co-workers, family, and friends. Amen.

Today's Reflection on Living, Loving, Leading

_____

_____

_____

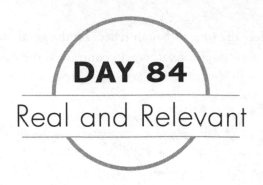

DAY 84
Real and Relevant

Today's Scripture

We have heard it with our ears, O God; our ancestors
have told us what you did in their days, in days long ago.
With your hand you drove out the nations and planted
our ancestors; you crushed the peoples and
made our ancestors flourish.

PSALM 44:1–2 NIV

I have a deep sense of gratitude for those who have partnered with Bobbie and me through all the seasons of church life: the highs and the lows, the joys and the sorrows, the seasons of momentum and utter frustration. But I have also seen way too many ministries age, blissfully unaware of their shrinking impact, influence, and relevance as their environment ages along with them. I'm determined not to allow that to happen with our ministry. We need to honor the past, but also build for the future. Connected to the world we live in, but positioned in a way that brings hope, love, and answers to people of all walks of life and experiences. In other words, keeping it real—and relevant.

People are not looking for stale religion; they want to know that God can make a difference in their lives, their families, their relationships, and their workplace today—and he can! If we have a generational focus in all that we do, our faith will continue to surge forward, and countless lives will continue to be indelibly changed. We will move into the future with a confidence in the ways God wants to grow the seeds of faith he has planted.

I was recently thinking about this in relation to Psalm 44 (especially the verse above). Here the sons of Korah reflect on the good old days, the days when God was with their forefathers, in contrast to the days they were living in now, when they felt God had forsaken them.

What will the coming generations say when they look back in history to the twenty-first century? Will they, like the sons of Korah, marvel at the move of God, the progress of the Church, and the advancement of the kingdom?

I certainly hope so. I believe we have a responsibility to the legend and legacy we will leave the coming generations. We have no control over how the future generations will steward what is given to them, but we can set them up to win by teaching them how to "Love God, Love People, and Love Life."

Today's Thought

If your earnest commitment as an individual believer and leader is fulfilling the Great Commission—sharing the gospel with everyone—and teaching others to do likewise, the Church will never fade into insignificance.

Today's Prayer

Dear Lord, thank you for the ways you are equipping me to fulfill your Great Commission. As I try to live, love, and lead like you, Jesus, I ask for your perspective on how I can make the most of all I've been given. Open my eyes to your eternal kingdom so that I may leave a faith legacy for future generations. Amen.

Today's Reflection on Living, Loving, Leading

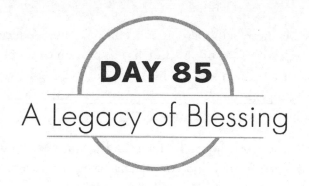

DAY 85

A Legacy of Blessing

Today's Scripture

One generation shall praise Your works to another,
and shall declare Your mighty acts.

PSALM 145:4 NKJV

Brenden grew up in the Catholic Church, yet at the age of fourteen, an older friend offered him drugs and alcohol at a party. Soon weekend after weekend, party after party, and substance after substance, his life spun out of control. By his early twenties Brenden was living recklessly, and his life felt empty. Lacking purpose, he became the manager of a nightclub where his destructive habits were not only fed but encouraged.

One night, at the young age of twenty-three, Brenden stumbled out of a nightclub after taking a lethal mixture of substances. He recalls how everything was spinning; he couldn't breathe and felt enveloped by the fear in his heart as he realized that he might be dying. Sitting down in a dirty gutter, empty bottles and garbage at his feet, he cried out, "God, if you're real, I'm scared. Please help me get out of this place—I'm too young to die!"

God not only answered his prayer, but over the next six months he brought people into Brenden's life who shared with him the story of God's love, hope, and redemption. People who loved him and told him that God also loved him, just the way he was. In March 2001, two of Brenden's friends invited him to attend church—our church. That night he encountered God and responded to the salvation altar call, opening his life to the saving work of Jesus Christ.

Over the next number of years, I had the privilege to watch Brenden not only change his lifestyle but also attend Hillsong Bible College and contribute so much to the life of our church. His passion to see other people's lives changed has led him to share his story and the gospel with countless others—including his own parents, his only brother, and ultimately the beautiful woman who became his wife.

I now watch with great joy as Brenden and Jacqui pastor our Burwood campus in western Sydney and continually bring new people to church; their two young sons worship with outstretched arms in our kids' programs, and their own families have not only found Jesus but also serve in the House of God. An entire family legacy changed by the powerful story of one encounter, one invitation, one decision!

Brenden's story reminds us that we must not simply build only for what we immediately see, but for the potential in generations unborn, those who have not yet met Jesus, who will one day sit in our seats, stand on our shoulders, and do greater things than we have ever done. We must leave a legacy of blessing.

Today's Thought

Make the decision right now to choose the pathway of blessing that God has laid out for you in the Bible, the Holy Calling, and the narrow gate, so that long after you have gone, your legacy of blessing will live on in the generations to come.

Today's Prayer

Dear God, it amazes me to hear stories like Brenden's and to see the ways you work in others' lives. Give me the courage to minister to those who are desperately in need and seeking you. I want to be your catalyst for change so that others may find new life, new joy, and new hope through the power of your Son. Thank you for loving me so much and using my life to draw others to you. Amen.

Today's Reflection on Living, Loving, Leading

DAY 86
A Glorious Future

Today's Scripture

*By faith Abraham, when called to go to a place he would
later receive as his inheritance, obeyed and went,
even though he did not know where he was going.*

HEBREWS 11:8 NIV

The church where I grew up in Lower Hutt, New Zealand, was a vibrant church with several hundred worshippers every Sunday morning—still, there was always one voice you could hear above every other: Granny Diamond. She was always a bar or two ahead of everyone else, and by the pitch and pace of her melodic hymns, you could always tell that Granny Diamond was in church, even though she was far too short to actually be seen!

When I first met Granny Diamond, she was elderly and tiny in stature—I think I outgrew her when I was about ten years old. She was frail and bent over, but boy did she have a good set of lungs!

I remember hearing a story about Granny Diamond that perfectly describes her posture of faith. Apparently, she collapsed on the railway station platform one day many years ago as she awaited her train home. Bystanders were quick to call the ambulance, and within minutes the medics were on the scene, kneeling over this tiny and seemingly fragile woman. But Granny Diamond didn't want a bar of it. Though she lay on the train platform gasping for breath, she began to sing and worship at the top of her lungs. Fighting off the bemused paramedics, she got to her feet and finally walked all the way home, still singing and praising her God.

Granny Diamond's faith was muscular, gutsy, and robust—the kind of faith that left an impression on a young boy. She finally died just short of turning a hundred years old, and I imagine all of heaven can hear her praising, slightly out of time and a little out of tune, but louder than all the heavenly host.

Robust faith has very little to do with physical stature or strength but everything to do with spiritual muscle. I'd imagine that Granny Diamond is among the character of the kind of people we find listed in Hebrews 11, often called the "Faith Hall of Fame." These people displayed the type of faith you need to enjoy all that awaits you in your God-given purpose, the type of faith needed to live saved, called, and fulfilling the glorious future for which you are graced.

———————○———————

Today's Thought

Living, loving, and leading like Jesus requires spiritual muscle
and robust faith—like Granny Diamond's and that of
all the saints before us.

Today's Prayer

*Dear Lord, I pray that I would have a robust, gutsy, muscular faith
like that of Granny Diamond. Don't let me settle for anything less
than your best for my life. Keep me focused on eternity so I can be free
to live a wide-open life of power, peace, and purpose. Amen.*

Today's Reflection on Living, Loving, Leading

_____

_____

_____

_____

_____

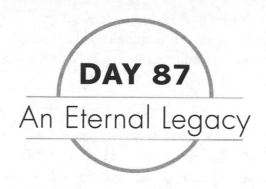

DAY 87
An Eternal Legacy

Today's Scripture

*Now faith is the substance of things hoped for,
the evidence of things not seen. For by it the elders
obtained a good testimony.*

HEBREWS 11:1–2 NKJV

Cataloging almost every incredible person and his or her story from the Old Testament, Hebrews 11 begins by simply defining its focus. These elders of the faith included Noah, Abraham and Sarah, Jacob, Joseph, Moses, Rahab, Samuel, and David, among many others. Their "good testimony" is the legacy of faith they left, the story of how they trusted God in the midst of overwhelming ordeals and obstacles.

Clearly, it wasn't their own power that fueled these individuals' victories. But it was actually out of their weaknesses that God enabled them to do amazing feats: conquer kingdoms, overcome lions, quench fires, dodge swords, and win battles when overwhelmingly outnumbered (Heb. 11:33–34). They found themselves in impossible situations and that's where God used them to reveal his presence, power, and purpose for all generations.

Sounds to me like pretty gutsy faith! I don't know about you, but I could often use courageous faith like that. Guts to share my faith, guts to do the right thing, guts to live well, lead well, and love well. Guts to stand up in the face of challenges and hold firm to God's promises.

The Bible frequently talks about this fight of faith. It's when you have no resources or opportunities, no solutions of your own, nowhere else to turn when you're in a battle, that you're forced to trust in God's ability to provide and meet you in your need. If nothing ever went wrong in life, then we wouldn't need to rely on faith or trust in God. We might as well be living in the Garden of Eden again.

But that's not where we are—we live in a world contaminated by human sin, a world of temptation and disappointment, a world that God saved through the gift of his Son's sacrifice on the cross. Daily we face unexpected challenges and overwhelming obstacles. But this is where God meets us. Therefore, we're called more than conquerors (Rom. 8:37), reflecting the truth that we are called to fight a battle of faith throughout our lives. Are you capable of that kind of faith? Are you ready and armed for the fight?

Today's Thought

Sometimes it's easy to have faith when everything is going
great, but courageous faith—robust faith—
is forged only when it's tested.

Today's Prayer

Dear Father God, help me to see the challenges and obstacles in my life right now as opportunities for courageous faith. Calm my fears and grant me your peace so that I may continue to step boldly into the future you have prepared for me. Amen.

Today's Reflection on Living, Loving, Leading

DAY 88
Moving Mountains

Today's Scripture

"Assuredly, I say to you, if you have faith and do not doubt, you will not only do what was done to the fig tree [he had just cursed and withered a fig tree], but also if you say to this mountain, 'Be removed and be cast into the sea,' it will be done. And whatever things you ask in prayer, believing, you will receive."

MATTHEW 21:21–22 NKJV

Here Jesus talks about faith that is strong enough to move mountains. Now that would take some strength! It's actually a pretty crazy thought. I don't know about you, but I would love to move a few mountains around. I used to love going snowboarding. I think one of the first things I would do with this kind of faith is move the biggest mountain in Australia (7,310 feet) to France, and I'd move the French Alps down to Australia. But I'm sure that's not what Jesus meant.

What he meant is that we will all encounter problems that become like mountains in our lifetime. Perhaps you can think of the mountains that are currently right in front of you. Maybe your mountains or your thirty-one kings have names like "debt," "marriage breakdown," "depression," or "cancer." We all face mountains that feel immoveable when we come up against them.

Sometimes our problems feel like a mountain filling the entire windshield of our car, obstructing the view and blocking our vision of the path ahead. The only remedy, the road map to traversing the rocky pass, coming around the last bend and seeing that mountain recede into the distance in your rearview mirror, is through holding on to God's Word and standing strong in your faith. These "mountain treks" are what testimonies are made of. What was once ahead of you, a seemingly impossibly large, rocky, slippery, and threatening mountain, has moved and is now behind you through the power that's in Jesus' name.

In more than thirty years of ministry, I've faced some serious mountains. I've come under fire from the press, faced disappointments with people, had a crisis of confidence, family challenges, and financial hurdles. Just like Joshua, I believe it is when there is land or territory at stake that faith comes with a fight. If you are facing a mountain, be encouraged—if you are gaining land, the devil is losing it, and the forces of darkness that are arraigned against God's promises hate losing territory.

Today's Thought

If you want to move mountains, true faith is the answer,
and robust and ready faith is the key.

Today's Prayer

*Dear Lord, I realize that my problems often feel like mountains,
when in fact, they are merely speed bumps along my path. Give me
the faith to move those mountains, regardless of their size, so that I
may persevere and run the race you have set for me and claim the
prize of spending eternity with you. Amen.*

Today's Reflection on Living, Loving, Leading

_____

_____

_____

_____

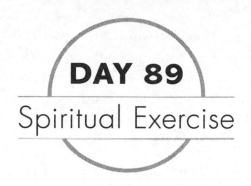

DAY 89
Spiritual Exercise

Today's Scripture

*"My grace is sufficient for you, for my power is made perfect
in weakness." Therefore I will boast all the more gladly about
my weaknesses, so that Christ's power may rest on me.*

2 CORINTHIANS 12:9 NIV

In order for our faith to endure over the long haul and in the midst of setbacks and challenges, we must exercise and strengthen it. The kind of faith required to survive life's harshest blows must be strong, muscular, robust, and resilient. The word *robust* means "strong and healthy; hardy and vigorous." Once we have made the commitment to follow Jesus and live the Christian life, we sometimes overlook our ongoing need to exercise and practice what we believe. But our spiritual muscles are very much like the ones in our bodies that need development on a regular basis in order to grow and remain strong and healthy.

Without regular physical exercise, our muscles atrophy—they shrink and weaken to the point that they no longer function properly. If we don't exercise our faith on a daily basis, then it becomes weak and limp, unable to stand up to the trials and temptations we inevitably face. We then feel discouraged and want to give up.

On the other hand, people who strengthen their faith and grow in their love and trust of God know that it requires practice. the right focus. They know we have to keep our faith in Jesus, not in other people or in material possessions or even in the Church. They know God will see them through every trial.

Grounded in your relationship with Christ, your faith grows over time with every new challenge, battle, or obstacle you face. You learn how to trust God beyond what you can see, feel, know, or even imagine. Especially when the unthinkable happens, then you have to trust God to provide something equally as unimaginable, something bigger than you can see from your current perspective.

Why would we be called overcomers if there was nothing to overcome? We would never be called more than conquerors if there were nothing to conquer, and if life never had any hurdles or challenges, faith would have no purpose. So, don't be dismayed when challenges come. Expect them to come and know that you have everything you need to conquer them—and then some.

Today's Thought

The Word of God says his strength is made perfect in our weakness (2 Cor. 12:9) and our faith will be refined by the fire (1 Pet. 1:7).

Today's Prayer

Dear Jesus, even though I know your strength is made perfect in my weakness, I sometimes struggle with feelings of doubt and uncertainty. Thank you for reminding me that these are only temporary and that you can use them to draw me closer to you. Keep me close to your heart, Lord, so that I may never wander from the path you have set for me. Amen.

Today's Reflection on Living, Loving, Leading

_____

_____

_____

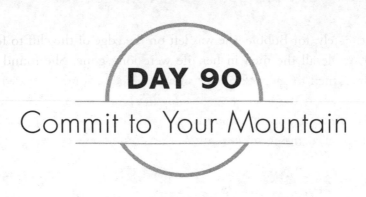

DAY 90
Commit to Your Mountain

Today's Scripture

I have fought the good fight, I have finished the race, I have kept the faith. Henceforth there is laid up for me the crown of righteousness, which the Lord, the righteous judge, will award to me on that Day, and not only to me but also to all who have loved his appearing.

2 TIMOTHY 4:7–8 ESV

Bobbie is probably the best skier in our family, but maybe that's because the rest of us snowboard—it's what us young people do. I may be the oldest and slowest snowboarder on the mountain, but our boys make up for my lack with their prowess. I initially took up snowboarding with the noble but naive intention of spending more quality time with them.

On one occasion, our boys lured Bobbie and me up the ski lift to a particularly high mountain peak. As we alighted the mountaintop, Bobbie was clearly unsure, but our sons can be very persuasive, and we united in our commitment to whatever lay ahead of us. We set out together, but after heading several hundred meters down a relatively easy early slope, everything began to change. The black diamonds on the marker sign were insight into the perilous path ahead.

It was already too late to make our way back to the lift, and before long we were standing on the edge of a virtual cliff with a breathtaking sheer drop. This provided no real challenge for the boys, who were beyond it in a moment and had disappeared through the tree line, as was normally the way. Somehow, I also miraculously managed to traverse my way down, negotiating the dangers and making my way to safer ground.

Unfortunately, for Bobbie, she was left on the edge of the cliff to fend for herself, while all the men in her life were long gone. She found herself literally pinned to the wall of this snow-covered mountain, knowing that she had nowhere to go but down! Seeing her hesitation and understanding her fear, a man stopped alongside her, took a look at the cliff, and said, "Ma'am, you've just got to commit to the mountain."

So that was exactly what she did. Ultimately my brave wife made her way back to the base healthy and intact, with a story to tell.

So many times in life are like trying to ski over the edge of a steep precipice when you can't see a path down. There's no way to turn back and no way to go forward. You feel stuck and afraid, at a loss for hope. These are the times when you must exercise your faith like never before, stepping into the glorious future God has for you even though you can't see what's ahead. There are times in life when you just have to commit to your mountain.

Today's Thought

Sometimes, when you feel cornered by life, hemmed in by less than ideal circumstances, you have to take that leap of faith, trusting that God will guide you and lead you through the trials and temptations you're facing.

Today's Prayer

Dear Jesus, I'm committed to following in your footsteps as I enjoy living, loving, and leading by your example. Give me the strength and courage to commit to the mountains that I encounter. I know I can do all things through you. Thank you for deepening my faith through these readings and my reflections on them. I feel both refreshed and equipped to tackle any obstacle on this adventure of faith we're on together. Our best is yet to come! Amen.

Today's Reflection on Living, Loving, Leading

LET'S TALK LEADERSHIP

Stay tuned for more leadership resources from Pastor Brian Houston, INCLUDING "Let's Talk Leadership" and "Let's Talk Church"—a series designed to empower leaders from all walks of life and levels of influence.

For over 40 years, Pastor Brian Houston has endeavored to preach to people's "Monday's" and not just their Sundays. Meaning, his life and leadership is all about empowering people to fulfill their unique purpose and calling—taking the principles that they learn in church and enabling them to outwork these practical lessons in their home, workplace, and relationships.

Many have described him as leading the charge in generational leadership, creating a diverse and accessible intersection of church and culture. He is a sought after teacher and speaker and is regarded as one of the foremost voices on leadership and the local church.

For more information and to stay up to date with
Brian Houston, Hillsong Church, and Let's Talk Leadership,
visit **brianandbobbie.com** or connect through
social media below.

Follow Brian on Twitter: **@BrianCHouston**

Follow Brian on Instagram: **@BrianCHouston**

Like Brian & Bobbie on Facebook:
facebook.com/BrianAndBobbie

MORE RESOURCES

There are various resources available, including more inspiring teaching and books by Brian Houston, to equip and empower you to lead in every area of your life.

No Other Name
Teaching Series

It is more than a clever slogan, a religious ritual, or an album title. The declaration that there is "No Other Name" has caused our hearts to rise up with faith and our voices to shout in unity as these messages have encouraged, strengthened, and set free. Join Pastor Brian Houston and Hillsong Church as we fall deeper in love with the power, authority, and presence of NO OTHER NAME than the name of JESUS.

My Spirit, My Responsibility
Teaching, Healthy Leadership Culture

My Spirit, My Responsibility explores what it means to take personal responsibility for what thoughts and meditations govern our spirit, as we walk through life's failures, successes, partnerships and relationships, and endeavor to live a life that is obedient to Jesus Christ.

Healthy Leadership Culture
Leadership Lessons from Hillsong Staff Meetings

Each week, Pastor Brian gathers the collective staff of Hillsong Church and empowers them with practical tools and leadership lessons that will not only build the church, but build their lives. From building a healthy home to building a healthy culture, he unpacks how to develop the responsibility of "culture carriers" into your team and congregation alike.

AVAILABLE AT HILLSONG.COM/STORE

PODCASTS

Each and every day, thousands of people are accessing FREE audio podcasts from Pastor Brian Houston. These messages are created to bring hope and encouragement, to inspire generations of believers with practical and biblical teaching. Your work life, home life, and relationships matter to God—and they matter to us. Join thousands of others to receive free teaching that will unlock and unleash you to your greatest potential.

To access and subscribe to these life-giving messages, search for "Brian Houston" in the iTunes Store or Podcast App.

HILLSONG TV
WITH BRIAN HOUSTON

Each week, millions of people from 160 countries around the world tune into Hillsong Television with Brian Houston—a half-hour program straight from the platform of Hillsong Church. We receive letters every day from people whose lives have changed through the Word of God broadcast through their television screens—from the most remote villages to prison cells and living rooms, the gospel message of Jesus Christ is transforming lives. Join Pastor Brian Houston and Hillsong Church by watching youtube.com/hillsongchurchtv or visiting hillsongtv.com to see which channel Hillsong Television is broadcast on in your local area.

MY MISSION

It was in 1993 when I sat down to write out a vision—a dream in my heart for a church that I longed to pastor. What I penned was indeed a visionary statement and a long way from the reality that we experienced then. By the grace of God, in many ways that vision, "The Church That I See," beautifully describes what God has built in our midst and perfectly encapsulates what many know today as Hillsong Church.

So it was on our 30th anniversary as a church in 2014 that I sat down once again to dream, pray, cast vision, and write a new and daring mission statement that would launch us—a now global church—into the next season of God's faithfulness and fruitfulness, and set the platform for generations to come...

THE CHURCH I NOW SEE

The church that I see is a global church. I see a global family: One house with many rooms, outworking a unified vision. I see a church apostolic in calling and visionary in nature; committed to boldly impacting millions for Christ in significant cities and nations throughout the earth with the greatest of all causes—the Cause of our Lord Jesus Christ.

I see a church that champions the cause of local churches everywhere, encouraging them to be all that God has called them to be. A church that refuses to be content with the triumphs of the past, but is constantly looking toward the future—filled with a vision that inspires and influences many.

Positioned in the heart of culture, in great diverse urban centers, I see buildings that struggle to contain the increase of all that God is doing; occupying land and places that are miraculous in provision and impossible to ignore.

I see a church that is big enough to dream on a global scale, yet personal enough for every ONE to find their place. I see a church that beckons "WELCOME HOME" to every man, woman, and child who walks through the doors.

The church that I see is a worshipping church whose songs reflect such a passion for Christ that others sense His magnificence and power. A distinct sound that emanates from a healthy church, contagious in spirit—creating music that resounds from villages and tribes to great cities and nations.

I see a church that is constantly innovative: A church that leads the communication of a timeless message through media, film, and technology. A church with a message beamed to people around the globe through their television screens, bringing JESUS into homes, palaces and prisons alike.

I see a church with a world-class college that raises, equips, and empowers generations of young, anointed leaders from across the globe. Graduates who serve God in all walks of life, released to salt the earth with dynamic ministries and churches throughout the continents of the world.

I see a church graced with layers of "once-in-a-generation" type leaders, who are naturally gifted, spiritually potent, and genuinely humble. Leaders who will pay the price and count the cost of impacting cities and nations with great, God-glorifying churches.

I see a church whose leadership is unified in their commitment to the authenticity, credibility, and quality of its heart. Leaders who dare to be themselves, yet live secure in the knowledge that "what they are part of is bigger than the part they play."

I see a church committed to an innovative NETWORK that connects hundreds of thousands of pastors and leaders and equips them to flourish. A network committed to the apostolic anointing of leaders who are desperate to see the Church of Jesus Christ rise up to live the un-lived life within her...His glorious Church.

I see like-spirited churches in cities of influence that exemplify faithfulness manifested in bricks and mortar. Churches with supernatural provision of buildings and properties standing as beacons of light that bring glory to God and hope to humanity.

I see a church that loves God, loves people, and loves life. Youthful in spirit, generous at heart, faith-filled in confession, loving in nature, and inclusive in expression.

Yes, the church that I see is committed to bringing the love and hope of Christ to impossible situations through the preaching of the gospel and a mandate that drives us to do all we can to bring help and solution to a needy world. Whose head is Jesus, help is the Holy Spirit, and whose focus is the Great Commission.

—Brian Houston 2014